I0696941

HOW TO OVERCOME INSECURITY

DAVID SANDUA

How to overcome insecurity.

Kindle Direct Publishing
Paperback Edition 2023

"To overcome fear is the quickest way to gain your self-confidence."

Roy T. Bennett

INDEX

I. INTRODUCTION

In today's highly competitive and interconnected society, it is not uncommon for individuals to experience feelings of insecurity and self-doubt. These feelings can be detrimental to one's personal and professional growth, hindering their ability to reach their full potential. Overcoming insecurity is not an insurmountable task; it requires self-reflection, a proactive approach, and a willingness to step out of one's comfort zone. This essay aims to explore the complexities of insecurity and provide practical strategies to help individuals overcome this common challenge. Insecurity can manifest in various aspects of an individual's life, such as relationships, career, and self-perception. This sense of inadequacy often stems from comparing oneself to others and feeling as though we fall short in some way. Social media platforms, for instance, exacerbate this problem by constantly bombarding us with images of others' seemingly perfect lives and achievements, which can make us feel inadequate and further perpetuate our insecurities. Societal expectations and cultural norms place a considerable amount of pressure on individuals to conform to certain standards, which can contribute to feelings of self-doubt and inferiority.

To overcome insecurity, it is essential to first understand the root causes of these feelings and challenge negative thought patterns. Self-reflection plays a crucial role in this process, as it allows individuals to examine their beliefs and behaviors that contribute to insecurity. By identifying the specific triggers and patterns that fuel these feelings, individuals can begin to develop a deeper understanding of themselves and their insecurities.

This self-awareness is a vital step towards overcoming feelings of inadequacy and building self-confidence.

Taking a proactive approach to tackle insecurity entails engaging in activities that foster personal growth and self-improvement. This can involve setting realistic goals and working towards achieving them, whether it is in academic, professional, or personal spheres. By focusing on one's own progress and striving for personal milestones, individuals can shift their attention away from comparisons with others and develop a sense of confidence in their own abilities. Continuous learning and seeking new experiences can also help individuals expand their comfort zones and build resilience in the face of challenges. In addition, seeking support from others is crucial in the journey of overcoming insecurity. Friends, family, or mentors can provide valuable guidance and encouragement, reminding individuals of their strengths and helping them reframe their negative self-perceptions. Surrounding oneself with positive influences and a support network can greatly contribute to developing a healthy self-image and boosting self-esteem. Therapy or counseling sessions can provide a safe and non-judgmental environment for individuals to explore their insecurities and develop effective coping mechanisms.

While insecurity is a common experience, it is not insurmountable. Overcoming insecurity requires self-reflection, a proactive approach, and a willingness to seek support from others.

By challenging negative thought patterns, setting achievable goals, and surrounding oneself with positive influences, individuals can gradually overcome their insecurities and cultivate a healthy sense of self-worth. The strategies discussed in this essay serve as a starting point for individuals seeking to overcome insecurity and ultimately unleash their true potential.

DEFINITION OF INSECURITY

Insecurity can be defined as a deep-seated feeling of inadequacy, doubt, self-doubt, or fear of judgment. It is the persistent belief that one is not good enough, capable enough, or worthy enough. Insecurity can manifest in various aspects of life, including personal relationships, academic pursuits, and professional endeavors. It often stems from past experiences, societal pressures, or negative self-perceptions. Insecure individuals constantly compare themselves to others, focusing on their perceived flaws and failures rather than their strengths and achievements. This preoccupation with self-doubt often leads to a cycle of negative thoughts and behaviors, further reinforcing their feelings of insecurity. Insecurity is not a constant state, but rather fluctuates depending on the circumstances and the individual's internal state. It can be temporary, triggered by a specific event or interaction, or it may be a chronic, long-standing issue that affects every aspect of one's life. There are different types of insecurity, such as physical insecurity, where individuals are dissatisfied with their appearance and believe they do not meet societal standards of beauty or attractiveness. Another type is social insecurity, where individuals constantly worry about their social interactions and fear being judged or criticized by others. This type of insecurity often leads to seeking validation and approval from others in order to feel accepted and valued. There is academic insecurity, which is characterized by a lack of confidence in one's intellectual abilities, often resulting in low self-esteem and a fear of failure. Insecurity can also extend to professional settings, where individuals may feel insecure about their skills, knowledge, or how they compare to their colleagues. This can lead to self-sabotaging behaviors such as avoiding new opportunities or settling for mediocrity due to the fear of failure. Insecurity can have a profound impact on an individual's mental and emotional well-being. It can create a constant inner turmoil, leading to anxiety, depression, and a diminished sense of self-worth. Insecurity can also hinder personal growth and development, as individuals are too preoccupied with their perceived shortcomings to take risks or pursue their goals wholeheartedly. It can strain relationships, as the constant need for reassurance and validation can become exhausting for both parties involved. Overcoming insecurity requires a multifaceted approach that addresses the underlying causes and cultivates self-acceptance and self-compassion. It involves challenging negative beliefs and thought patterns, replacing them with positive and realistic ones. Developing a strong support system of trusted individuals who provide encouragement and constructive feedback can also help build confidence and resilience. Engaging in self-care activities that promote self-compassion and self-awareness, such as meditation, Mindfulness, and therapy, can aid in the journey of overcoming insecurity. By actively working towards a healthier mindset and building a foundation of self-acceptance and self-love, individuals can gradually break free from the grips of insecurity and embrace their true potential.

PREVALENCE OF INSECURITY AMONG INDIVIDUALS

Insecurity is a prevalent issue that affects individuals from all walks of life. Research has shown that a significant portion of the population experiences some degree of insecurity, whether it is related to their appearance, abilities, or social status. One of the reasons for the prevalence of insecurity is the constant comparison that individuals engage in due to the pervasive nature of social media. Today, individuals are bombarded with images and stories of seemingly perfect lives, which can lead to feelings of inadequacy and insecurity. The pressure to conform to societal beauty standards, achieve professional success, or maintain a certain lifestyle can be overwhelming and contribute to individuals feeling insecure about themselves. Societal expectations and norms play a significant role in perpetuating feelings of insecurity. From a young age, individuals are often told what they should or should not look like, how they should behave, and what success should look like. These expectations can create a constant fear of not meeting the standards set by society, thus leading to a sense of insecurity. In addition to societal pressures, personal experiences and traumas also contribute to the prevalence of insecurity. Past experiences, such as bullying, abusive relationships, or failures, can leave lasting scars and make individuals doubt their worth and abilities. These experiences often shape an individual's self-perception, making them more susceptible to feelings of insecurity. The fear of judgment and rejection also plays a significant role in the prevalence of insecurity. Individuals may fear being ridiculed or rejected by their peers, families, or communities if they do not meet certain expectations. This fear can prevent individuals from fully expressing themselves and pursuing their goals, leading to a constant sense of insecurity. The need for validation and acceptance is a common contributing factor to the prevalence of insecurity. Human beings have an inherent desire to be liked and accepted by others. Unfortunately, this need for external validation can become a source of insecurity. Individuals may constantly seek approval from others, doubting their own worth and relying on the opinions of others to feel secure. This constant need for validation can be exhausting and perpetuate feelings of insecurity. Insecurity is a prevalent issue that affects individuals at various stages of their lives. The constant comparison fueled by social media, societal expectations and norms, personal experiences and traumas, fear of judgment and rejection, and the need for validation and acceptance are all contributing factors to the prevalence of insecurity. Overcoming insecurity requires a deep understanding and acceptance of oneself, challenging societal norms and expectations, seeking support and therapy to address past traumas, and cultivating self-confidence and self-worth. By addressing these underlying causes and taking proactive steps towards personal growth and self-acceptance, individuals can overcome insecurity and lead fulfilling lives.

IMPORTANCE OF OVERCOMING INSECURITY

Overcoming insecurity is critical for personal growth and development. Insecurity can severely hinder an individual's ability to take risks and try new things. It creates a constant fear of failure and judgement, leading to a stagnant and limited life. By stepping out of our comfort zones and facing our insecurities head-on, we can experience tremendous personal growth. Overcoming insecurities allows us to challenge ourselves, set ambitious goals, and pursue our passions without the fear of failure or judgement. This opens up a world of opportunities and possibilities, allowing us to reach our fullest potential.

In addition, overcoming insecurity is essential for building and nurturing relationships. Insecurity often leads to excessive self-focus, causing individuals to become overly anxious about how others perceive them. This self-centered approach creates barriers in forming meaningful connections with others.

Insecure individuals may struggle with trust and vulnerability, preventing them from forming deep and intimate relationships. When we work towards overcoming our insecurities, we become more open and authentic in our interactions with others. We are able to let go of our fears of being judged or rejected, allowing us to genuinely connect with others on a deeper level. By being vulnerable and showing our true selves, we invite others to do the same, fostering trust and deepening relationships. Overcoming insecurity not only improves our relationships with others but also enhances our own self-worth and sense of belonging.

Overcoming insecurity is crucial for mental and emotional well-being. Insecurity often leads to negative self-talk and self-doubt, which can take a toll on our mental and emotional health. It creates a constant state of anxiety and stress, leaving individuals feeling overwhelmed and exhausted. By challenging these negative thoughts and beliefs, we can gain control over our emotions and improve our overall well-being. Overcoming insecurity allows us to cultivate self-compassion and self-acceptance, enabling us to develop a positive and resilient mindset. It frees us from the chains of self-imposed limitations and empowers us to pursue a fulfilling and meaningful life.

Overcoming insecurity is crucial in the professional realm. Insecurity can hinder career advancement by limiting our confidence and ability to take on new challenges and opportunities. It instills a fear of failure and a lack of belief in our abilities, preventing us from reaching our full potential in the workplace. When we address and overcome our insecurities, we are able to cultivate confidence, resilience, and a growth mindset. We become more willing to take risks, embrace change, and pursue new professional endeavors. Overcoming insecurity not only enhances our performance but also allows us to build professional networks, seek guidance, and learn from others. It enables us to seize opportunities, advance in our careers, and achieve professional success. Overcoming insecurity is of vital importance for personal growth, building relationships, maintaining mental and emotional well-being, and achieving professional success. Overcoming insecurities allows individuals to step out of their comfort zones, pursue their passions fearlessly, and reach their fullest potential. It fosters deep and meaningful connections with others, enhances self-worth, and promotes a positive and resilient mindset. Overcoming insecurity in the professional realm empowers individuals to take risks, embrace change, and achieve success. It is through addressing and overcoming our insecurities that we can truly unlock our true potential and live a fulfilling and meaningful life.

Another effective way to overcome insecurity is to practice self-compassion. Individuals who struggle with insecurity are extremely hard on themselves, constantly criticizing and belittling their own abilities and worth. This negative self-talk only perpetuates the feelings of inadequacy and self-doubt, making it even more difficult to break free from the cycle of insecurity. It is crucial to cultivate self-compassion by being kind and understanding towards oneself. This involves treating oneself with the same empathy and compassion that one would show to a loved one in times of distress. Instead of berating oneself for any perceived flaws or mistakes, one should strive to practice self-forgiveness and understanding. Acknowledging that nobody is perfect and that it is natural to make mistakes can help alleviate the burden of insecurity. It is important to remind oneself of one's positive qualities and accomplishments, no matter how small they may seem. This can be done by writing down affirmations or listing one's achievements in a journal. By regularly reminding oneself of these positive aspects, one can gradually build up self-esteem and confidence, which are essential in overcoming insecurity. Engaging in self-care activities can also contribute to self-compassion. Taking the time to relax, pursue hobbies, or engage in activities that bring joy and fulfillment can help shift the focus away from insecurities and onto self-nurturing. Whether it is reading a book, going for a walk in nature, or practicing Mindfulness, finding activities that promote self-care can greatly boost one's sense of self-worth and alleviate insecurity. Practicing self-compassion is not an overnight solution but rather a lifelong journey. It requires consistent effort and patience, as breaking free from insecurity is a process that takes time and dedication. By adopting a mindset of self-compassion, individuals can gradually overcome their insecurities and develop a healthier and more positive relationship with themselves. Insecurity is a common struggle that can greatly hinder personal growth and well-being.

It is not an insurmountable obstacle. By challenging negative beliefs, seeking support from loved ones and professionals, and practicing self-compassion, individuals can gradually overcome their insecurities and lead more fulfilling lives. The journey to overcoming insecurity may be difficult, but with perseverance and a commitment to self-improvement, it is entirely possible. It is important to remember that everyone deserves to feel secure and confident in themselves, and by taking these steps, one can take the first crucial steps towards achieving that goal.

II. UNDERSTANDING INSECURITY

Insecurity can manifest in various ways and affect individuals in different areas of their lives. One aspect of insecurity is the fear of rejection, which can lead individuals to constantly seek approval and validation from others. They may feel an overwhelming need to please others and become overly sensitive to criticism or perceived rejection. This fear of rejection can also result in individuals avoiding social interactions or new experiences, as they fear being judged or rejected by others. A lack of self-confidence is another common manifestation of insecurity. Individuals who lack confidence may constantly doubt themselves and their abilities, believing that they are not capable of achieving their goals or deserving of success. This can be debilitating and prevent individuals from taking risks or pursuing opportunities. Insecurity can also manifest in relationships, causing individuals to have a fear of intimacy or commitment. They may struggle to trust others and constantly seek reassurance and confirmation of their partner's love and loyalty. This can lead to a cycle of neediness and dependency, which can put strain on the relationship. Individuals who feel insecure may develop a strong need for control, as they believe that maintaining control over their surroundings and relationships will provide them with a sense of security. They may become overly possessive or jealous, creating tension and conflict within their relationships. Insecurity can also give rise to negative self-talk and a critical inner voice. Individuals may constantly berate themselves, focusing on their flaws and shortcomings. This negative self-talk further erodes their self-esteem and reinforces their feelings of insecurity. Individuals who are insecure may engage in self-sabotaging behaviors. They may deliberately fail to avoid taking risks or setting high expectations, as they fear failure and the negative judgments of others. This can become a self-fulfilling prophecy, as their lack of confidence and belief in themselves leads to missed opportunities and unrealized potential. Understanding the various manifestations of insecurity is crucial in overcoming it. Individuals need to recognize that insecurity is not a fixed characteristic but a learned behavior rooted in personal experiences and beliefs. By identifying the ways in which insecurity manifests in one's life, individuals can begin to challenge and reframe their thoughts and behaviors. This may involve seeking support from trusted friends or professionals, who can provide guidance and help individuals develop healthier coping mechanisms. Fostering self-compassion and acceptance is crucial in overcoming insecurity. By cultivating self-compassion, individuals can learn to embrace their imperfections and recognize their worth beyond external validation. With time and effort, it is possible to overcome insecurity and develop a sense of self-assurance and self-worth. By understanding insecurity and its various manifestations and taking proactive steps towards healing and growth, individuals can break free from the limitations that insecurity imposes and achieve a more fulfilling and confident life.

FACTORS CONTRIBUTING TO INSECURITY: PAST EXPERIENCES AND SOCIETAL PRESSURES

Another factor that contributes to insecurity is societal pressures. Society often sets standards and expectations for individuals to meet. These expectations can be related to one's appearance, success, relationships, or social status. When individuals feel that they do not meet these expectations or they do not fit into the societal norms, they may develop feelings of inadequacy and insecurity. Society creates a constant pressure to live up to certain ideals, which can be overwhelming for many individuals. For example, the media often portrays an image of beauty and success that is difficult to achieve, leading individuals to compare themselves and feel insecure about their own appearance or achievements. Societal pressures can also include expectations from family, friends, and acquaintances. These expectations can range from academic and career achievements to conforming to traditional gender roles or cultural norms. For instance, in some cultures, there may be societal expectations for individuals to get married at a certain age, have a successful career, or have children. Failure to meet these expectations can result in feelings of insecurity and self-doubt. Societal pressures can also stem from social media, where individuals see curated versions of others' lives, which can lead to feelings of inadequacy and comparison. In today's digital age, individuals are constantly bombarded with images and messages that reinforce societal ideals and perpetuate insecurities. It is crucial to recognize the influence of societal pressures on one's sense of self-worth and take steps to counteract these negative effects. Building self-confidence and self-acceptance can help individuals navigate societal pressures and develop a more positive self-image. Past experiences and societal pressures are two major factors that contribute to insecurity. Past experiences such as traumatic events, bullying, or rejection can leave lasting emotional scars and affect an individual's sense of self. Similarly, societal pressures to meet certain standards and expectations, whether related to appearance, success, relationships, or social status, can lead to feelings of inadequacy and self-doubt. Overcoming insecurity requires individuals to reflect on their past experiences and recognize how these experiences have shaped their beliefs about themselves. It also involves challenging societal norms and expectations, understanding that these standards are often unrealistic and do not define one's worth. Developing self-compassion, building self-confidence, and practicing self-acceptance are essential steps towards overcoming insecurity. Seeking support from trusted individuals, such as friends, family members, or professionals, can provide valuable guidance and encouragement throughout this journey. It is important to remember that insecurity is a common human experience, and it is possible to move beyond it with time, patience, and self-reflection. By addressing the factors contributing to insecurity and actively working towards self-acceptance, individuals can cultivate a more positive and confident sense of self and lead a more fulfilling and empowered life.

IMPACT OF INSECURITY ON PERSONAL AND PROFESSIONAL LIFE

Insecurity can wreak havoc on both personal and professional aspects of an individual's life, leading to a multitude of negative consequences. On a personal level, insecurity can greatly hinder one's ability to form and maintain healthy relationships. Constantly doubting oneself and feeling unworthy can make it difficult to open up to others, trust them, and establish genuine connections. This can create a perpetual cycle of isolation, as individuals may feel too insecure to reach out for support or fear being rejected by others. The fear of judgment and criticism can prevent individuals from pursuing their passions and taking risks, leading to a stagnant personal growth and an inability to fully explore their interests and talents.

Similarly, the impact of insecurity on one's professional life can be profound. Insecurities can impede an individual's career progression, as they may doubt their abilities and shy away from opportunities for advancement. The fear of failure or being exposed as a fraud can hinder individuals from taking on new challenges and responsibilities, limiting their potential for growth and development within their field. Insecurity can hinder effective communication and collaboration with colleagues, as individuals may constantly second-guess their ideas and contributions. This can lead to missed opportunities for innovation and creativity within the workplace, ultimately hindering both individual and organizational success.

Insecurity can significantly impact an individual's mental health and overall well-being. The constant self-doubt and negative self-talk that accompanies insecurity can lead to increased levels of stress, anxiety, and even depression. The fear of failure and constant comparison to others can create a perpetual state of distress, making it difficult for individuals to find peace and contentment in their lives. Insecurity can fuel a vicious cycle of seeking external validation, as individuals may become overly reliant on others' opinions and approval to feel a sense of self-worth. This dependency can ultimately erode one's sense of self and lead to a loss of personal identity.

The impact of insecurity on personal and professional life is multifaceted and far-reaching. It can hinder the formation of meaningful relationships, impede career progression, and negatively affect one's mental health. It is essential to recognize that insecurity is not an inherent characteristic of an individual but rather a learned behavior that can be unlearned through self-reflection, therapy, and conscious efforts to challenge negative thought patterns. By confronting and addressing insecurities head-on, individuals can embark on a journey of self-discovery and personal growth, enabling them to lead more fulfilling and successful lives both personally and professionally. It is crucial to remember that everyone experiences insecurities to some extent, and it is through embracing vulnerability and seeking support that individuals can cultivate resilience and overcome the negative impact of insecurity on their lives.

RECOGNIZING THE SIGNS OF INSECURITY IN ONESELF AND OTHERS

Recognizing the signs of insecurity both in oneself and others is essential for personal growth and maintaining healthy relationships. In oneself, insecurity can manifest in numerous ways. First and foremost, individuals may constantly doubt their own abilities and worth, leading to a lack of self-confidence.

This can be observed when individuals are hesitant to take on new challenges or goals, fearing failure or judgment from others. Individuals who are insecure may have a constant need for validation from others, seeking reassurance and approval in order to feel secure about themselves. They may also develop a habit of comparing themselves to others, constantly feeling inferior and envious of the accomplishments and qualities of those around them. Another sign of insecurity in oneself lies in the fear of rejection and abandonment. Individuals who struggle with insecurity often have difficulty forming deep and meaningful connections, as they are afraid of being hurt or rejected by others. These individuals may also exhibit a tendency to over-analyze interactions and seek for hidden meanings in every word and action, magnifying their anxiety and self-doubt. On the other hand, recognizing signs of insecurity in others can enable us to provide support and encouragement to those who need it. Insecure individuals may exhibit similar patterns of behavior as mentioned earlier, such as constantly seeking approval, comparing themselves to others, and fearing rejection. They may also display a lack of assertiveness, finding it difficult to voice their opinions and desires out of fear of judgment or disapproval. It is important to approach individuals with empathy and understanding, as insecurity can profoundly impact their self-esteem and overall well-being. Recognizing signs of insecurity in others can help us navigate interactions and communication more effectively. Insecure individuals may often display defensive behaviors when faced with criticism or perceived threats to their self-worth. Understanding that these behaviors stem from their own insecurities can prevent misunderstandings and allow for more constructive conversations. Recognizing signs of insecurity can enable us to create a safe and supportive environment for others, where they feel encouraged to express their vulnerabilities and work towards building their self-confidence. Recognizing the signs of insecurity in oneself and others is an essential step towards personal growth and fostering healthy relationships. By identifying these signs, individuals can take proactive measures to address their own insecurities, such as seeking therapy or practicing self-compassion. When it comes to others, recognizing signs of insecurity can help us provide the necessary support and empathy to those who may be struggling with their self-esteem. Through understanding and patience, we can create an environment that encourages personal growth and empowerment, allowing individuals to overcome their insecurities and thrive. Another effective strategy to overcome insecurity is by challenging our negative self-talk and replacing it with positive affirmations. Oftentimes, our insecurities stem from the negative beliefs and thoughts we have about ourselves. We may constantly criticize ourselves, compare ourselves to others, or believe that we are not good enough. By challenging these negative thoughts and replacing them with positive affirmations, we can start to shift our mindset and build self-confidence. For example, instead of telling ourselves that we are not smart enough for a particular task, we can remind ourselves of our past achievements and capabilities. By consistently practicing positive self-talk, we can rewire our brains to focus on our strengths and reassess our self-worth. In addition to challenging our negative self-talk, it is crucial to surround ourselves with a supportive network of friends and family. Having a strong support system can provide us with the encouragement, validation, and constructive feedback that we need to overcome our insecurities. When we are surrounded by individuals who genuinely believe in us and celebrate our accomplishments, it becomes easier to silence the critical voice in our heads and embrace our worthiness. Supportive relationships can also serve as a source of inspiration and motivation, as we witness others successfully overcoming their own insecurities. By leaning on our support system during times of doubt, we can gather the strength and resilience to confront our insecurities head-on. It is important to foster self-acceptance and practice self-care as a means of overcoming insecurity. Insecurities often arise from a deep-rooted dissatisfaction with ourselves or a desire to meet unattainable standards set by society. Acceptance of our unique qualities, flaws, and imperfections is essential for true self-worth. We must recognize that no one is perfect and that all individuals have their own insecurities. Engaging in self-care activities can also help boost our confidence and self-esteem. Taking care of our physical, mental, and emotional well-being allows us to prioritize self-love and develop a positive relationship with ourselves. Whether it is engaging in yoga, practicing Mindfulness, or pursuing a hobby, investing time in activities that make us feel good about ourselves can have a profound impact on our overall sense of self. Overcoming insecurity requires dedication, self-reflection, and the adoption of various strategies. By challenging our negative self-talk, seeking support from our network, fostering self-acceptance, and practicing self-care, we can gradually alleviate our insecurities and develop a healthier sense of self-worth. It is important to remember that overcoming insecurity is an ongoing process and may require continuous effort and commitment. By actively taking steps to confront and address our insecurities, we can embark on a journey towards self-discovery, personal growth, and the realization of our true potential.

III. BUILDING SELF-AWARENESS

It involves recognizing and understanding one's thoughts, emotions, strengths, and weaknesses. Through self-awareness, individuals gain a deeper understanding of who they are, what they value, and how they interact with others. One way to build self-awareness is through reflection and introspection. Taking the time to reflect on one's experiences, thoughts, and feelings can provide valuable insights into patterns of behavior and triggers for insecurity. Journaling can be a helpful tool in this process, allowing individuals to record their thoughts and emotions, and identify any recurring themes. Practicing Mindfulness and meditation can cultivate a heightened sense of self-awareness. By intentionally focusing on the present moment and observing one's thoughts and emotions without judgment, individuals can gain a clearer understanding of their internal experiences. Another aspect of building self-awareness is seeking external feedback. Trusted friends, family members, or mentors can provide valuable perspectives on one's strengths, weaknesses, and blind spots. Engaging in honest conversations and actively listening to others' observations and suggestions can expand one's self-awareness and provide new insights into areas for personal growth. Self-assessment tools, such as personality tests or career assessments, can provide valuable information about one's values, interests, and strengths. By understanding oneself better, individuals can make more informed decisions and align their goals and aspirations with their authentic selves. Building self-awareness involves examining and challenging negative beliefs and perceptions about oneself. Insecurity often stems from distorted or unrealistic self-perceptions, such as feeling unworthy or fearing judgment from others. Cognitive-behavioral techniques, such as cognitive restructuring, can help individuals challenge and reframe these negative beliefs. By identifying evidence that contradicts these beliefs or adopting a more balanced perspective, individuals can gradually weaken the power of insecurity. It is also crucial to acknowledge and celebrate achievements and successes. Regularly taking inventory of one's accomplishments and strengths can help counteract feelings of inadequacy and foster a more positive self-image. By reminding oneself of past achievements, individuals can shift their focus from their perceived flaws to their resilience and capacity for growth.

Building self-awareness requires practicing self-compassion. Insecurity often accompanies harsh self-criticism and comparison to others. Cultivating self-compassion involves treating oneself with kindness, understanding, and empathy.

By acknowledging that everyone has flaws and faces challenges, individuals can approach their insecurities with gentleness rather than judgment. Engaging in self-care activities, such as exercise, pursuing hobbies, or spending time with loved ones, can also foster self-com passion by honoring one's own needs and well-being. Building self-awareness is a dynamic and lifelong process that requires intentional effort and ongoing reflection. It enables individuals to recognize and challenge their insecurities, develop a realistic self-image, and cultivate compassion and acceptance toward oneself. By actively building self-awareness, individuals can gradually overcome insecurity and develop a stronger sense of self-worth.

EVALUATING PERSONAL STRENGTHS AND WEAKNESSES

Understanding one's strengths allows individuals to focus on their areas of expertise and build confidence in their abilities. For instance, if a person excels in public speaking, they can capitalize on this strength by seeking opportunities to engage in public speaking events. By doing so, they will not only improve their skills but also gain recognition and validation, which can significantly boost self-assurance. Recognizing weaknesses plays a crucial role in developing self-esteem and overcoming insecurities. Acknowledging areas that require improvement allows individuals to take proactive steps towards growth and self-development. For example, if a person struggles with time management, they can invest time in learning effective strategies for prioritizing tasks and managing their schedule. By tackling this weakness head-on, individuals can experience a profound sense of accomplishment and increase their self-belief. Evaluating weaknesses also helps individuals identify patterns or obstacles that may be contributing to their insecurities. By examining these challenges objectively, individuals can strategize and implement appropriate solutions to overcome them. Understanding personal strengths and weaknesses can assist individuals in setting realistic goals and expectations for themselves. It can be easy to compare oneself to others and feel inadequate, especially in today's highly competitive society. By evaluating personal strengths, individuals can determine what is attainable and within their reach. Setting achievable goals can significantly increase self-confidence and reduce feelings of insecurity. Evaluating personal strengths and weaknesses empowers individuals to seek support and collaborate with others. No person is an island, and seeking assistance from others can be immensely beneficial in overcoming personal insecurities. By recognizing their weaknesses, individuals can actively seek guidance from peers, mentors, or professionals who have expertise in those areas. This collaboration can provide valuable insights, advice, and resources to address one's insecurities effectively. Not only does seeking support help in overcoming insecurities, but it also fosters personal growth and learning. Evaluating personal strengths and weaknesses is an ongoing process that requires self-reflection and self-awareness. As individuals grow and evolve, their strengths and weaknesses may change too. It is essential to regularly assess and update one's evaluation to adapt to new circumstances and challenges. Embracing this continuous cycle of self-improvement fosters resilience and self-confidence, enabling individuals to overcome insecurities effectively. Evaluating personal strengths and weaknesses is pivotal in overcoming insecurity. By understanding one's strengths and leveraging them, individuals can build confidence and self-assurance. Similarly, by acknowledging weaknesses and taking proactive measures for improvement, individuals can overcome insecurities and experience personal growth. Evaluating personal strengths and weaknesses also assists in setting realistic goals, seeking support from others, and fostering self-reflection. Through this ongoing process of self-assessment and growth, individuals can gradually overcome insecurities and live a life of fulfillment and confidence.

IDENTIFYING NEGATIVE SELF-TALK PATTERNS

Negative self-talk refers to the ongoing negative thoughts or beliefs that individuals have about themselves and their abilities. These patterns of self-criticism can be deeply ingrained and can greatly impact one's self-esteem and overall sense of security. To tackle this issue, it is essential to become aware of our negative self-talk patterns and identify them when they arise. One way to do this is through self-reflection and introspection. Taking the time to reflect on our thoughts and feelings and questioning the validity of our negative beliefs can help us challenge and change our self-talk patterns. Journaling can be a useful tool in identifying negative self-talk patterns. By writing down our thoughts and feelings, we can better understand the patterns and themes that emerge from our inner dialogue. Seeking feedback from trusted friends or family members can provide valuable insights into our negative self-talk patterns that we may not be aware of. Sometimes, others can see things in us that we cannot see in ourselves. Their perspectives can help us become more conscious of the negative self-talk patterns that we may have overlooked. Paying attention to our body language and physical sensations can provide clues about our negative self-talk patterns. For instance, if we notice ourselves tensing up or experiencing physical symptoms of anxiety when having certain thoughts, it can indicate that these thoughts are linked to negative self-talk. By being attuned to these bodily signals, we can interrupt the negative self-talk patterns and consciously replace them with more positive and empowering thoughts. In addition, it is helpful to be mindful of our language and the words we use when talking to ourselves. The language we use can shape our thoughts and feelings, so it is important to avoid negative and self-deprecating language and instead use positive and affirming words to foster self-confidence and self-assurance. Seeking professional help, such as therapy or counseling, can be incredibly beneficial in identifying and addressing negative self-talk patterns. A qualified therapist can provide guidance and support in recognizing and challenging negative beliefs, helping individuals develop healthier self-talk patterns. Identifying negative self-talk patterns is an integral part of overcoming insecurity. Through self-reflection, journaling, seeking feedback, paying attention to our body language, being mindful of our language, and seeking professional help, we can become more aware of our negative self-talk patterns and work towards replacing them with more positive and empowering thoughts. By consistently practicing these strategies, individuals can gradually reduce their insecurities and cultivate a more confident and secure sense of self.

CULTIVATING MINDFULNESS TO OBSERVE AND REGULATE EMOTIONS

Mindfulness, derived from Buddhist practices, involves being fully present in the moment and aware of one's thoughts, feelings, and bodily sensations without judgment or attachment. By cultivating Mindfulness, individuals can develop a heightened sense of self-awareness, allowing them to observe their emotions objectively rather than being overwhelmed by them. This practice enables individuals to recognize when they are experiencing insecurity and understand the underlying causes. Rather than suppressing or avoiding these emotions, Mindfulness teaches individuals to lean into discomfort and examine their insecurities with compassion and curiosity. Through consistent practice, individuals can begin to recognize patterns and triggers related to their insecurity, allowing them to regulate their emotions more effectively. Mindfulness also provides individuals with a sense of distance from their insecurities, enabling them to detach from negative self-judgments and cultivate a greater sense of self-acceptance and self-compassion.

Developing Mindfulness helps individuals develop emotional resilience, which is key to overcoming insecurity. With Mindfulness, individuals can create space between their emotions and their responses, allowing them to choose more adaptive ways of coping with insecurity. Instead of reacting impulsively or defensively, individuals can respond thoughtfully and constructively to these emotions. Mindfulness also fosters the ability to reflect on past experiences and become aware of conditioned beliefs and thought patterns that contribute to insecurity. By recognizing and challenging these negative beliefs, individuals can reframe their mindset and cultivate a more positive and empowering perspective. In addition to the internal benefits, the cultivation of Mindfulness has been shown to improve interpersonal relationships and decrease conflict. When individuals are mindful, they become more present and attentive in their interactions with others, leading to more effective communication and empathy. By observing and regulating their own emotions, individuals are better equipped to understand and respond to the emotions of others. This heightened empathy and emotional intelligence contribute to building more secure and satisfying relationships, as individuals are able to navigate conflicts and address insecurities in a healthier manner.

To cultivate Mindfulness and regulate emotions, individuals can engage in various practices such as meditation, breathing exercises, and body scan awareness. These practices can be done individually or with the guidance of teachers or therapists who specialize in Mindfulness-based approaches. Individuals can incorporate Mindfulness into their daily lives by being intentional with their actions and paying attention to their thoughts and feelings as they go about their day. By making Mindfulness a habitual practice, individuals can increase their overall well-being and resilience, ultimately overcoming feelings of insecurity. Cultivating Mindfulness to observe and regulate emotions is an integral part of overcoming insecurity. By developing self-awareness and emotional resilience through Mindfulness practices, individuals can observe their emotions objectively, understand the underlying causes of their insecurity, and choose more adaptive responses. Mindfulness also fosters self-compassion and promotes positive relationships, contributing to overall well-being and fulfillment. With dedication and practice, anyone can harness the power of Mindfulness in their journey to overcome insecurity. Another effective strategy to overcome insecurity is practicing self-compassion. Self-com passion involves treating oneself with kindness, understanding, and empathy, especially when confronted with feelings of insecurity. In our society, there is often pressure to be perfect and constantly achieve high standards, which can contribute to feelings of inadequacy and self-doubt. By practicing self-compassion, individuals can learn to embrace their faults and imperfections, recognizing that they are only human. Self-compassion also involves cultivating a positive and supportive inner voice, rather than engaging in self-criticism and negative self-talk. Research has shown that individuals who practice self-compassion have higher levels of self-esteem and overall well-being, as they are more resilient and are able to bounce back from setbacks. Self-compassion allows individuals to form a healthier relationship with themselves, fostering self-acceptance and self-love.

In addition, developing a growth mindset can be instrumental in overcoming insecurity. A growth mindset involves the belief that one's abilities and qualities can be developed through dedication and effort. On the other hand, individuals with a fixed mindset believe that their abilities are fixed and unchangeable. By adopting a growth mindset, individuals are more likely to see challenges and setbacks as opportunities for growth and learning, rather than as personal failures. This mindset shift reduces the fear of failure and encourages individuals to take risks and step out of their comfort zones. As a result, individuals become more resilient and confident, as they understand that their worth is not tied solely to their achievements. Developing a growth mindset also requires embracing a process-oriented approach, where the focus is on progress and improvement rather than comparing oneself to others. This shift in perspective allows individuals to appreciate their journey and acknowledge their accomplishments, no matter how small they may seem.

Seeking support from friends, family, or mental health professionals can greatly assist in overcoming insecurity. Insecurities thrive in isolation, and by openly discussing them with trusted individuals, individuals can gain valuable insights and perspectives, as well as receive emotional support. Friends and family can provide a safe space for vulnerability and offer encouragement and reassurance. Seeking the help of mental health professionals, such as therapists or counselors, can provide individuals with professional guidance and tools to manage their insecurities effectively. Therapy can assist individuals in identifying the underlying causes of their insecurities and develop strategies for challenging negative thought patterns and building self-confidence. Belonging to a support group or participating in group therapy can allow individuals to connect with others who may be experiencing similar insecurities, fostering a sense of shared understanding and camaraderie.

Overcoming insecurities requires patience, self-reflection, and active effort. By challenging negative thought patterns, practicing self-compassion, developing a growth mindset, and seeking support from others, individuals can begin to break free from the grips of insecurity. It is important to remember that insecurity is a common human experience, and no one is exempt from feeling insecure at times. However, with these strategies, individuals can cultivate self-confidence, resilience, and self-love,

enabling them to embrace their uniqueness and live more fulfilling lives.

IV. ENHANCING SELF-ESTEEM

Self-esteem is defined as the overall subjective evaluation of one's own worth or value as a person. When individuals have high self-esteem, they see themselves as capable, competent, and deserving of love and success. On the other hand, low self-esteem can lead to feelings of inadequacy, self-doubt, and even self-loathing. Developing and enhancing self-esteem is crucial for overcoming insecurity. There are various strategies and techniques that can help individuals boost their self-esteem. First and foremost, it is important to challenge and replace negative self-talk. Individuals with low self-esteem engage in negative self-talk, criticizing themselves and their abilities. This negative internal dialogue only reinforces feelings of insecurity and inadequacy. By consciously challenging these negative thoughts and replacing them with positive and supportive self-talk, individuals can begin to shift their mindset and improve their self-esteem. Another way to enhance self-esteem is by setting achievable goals and celebrating small victories. When individuals set goals for themselves and achieve them, they gain a sense of accomplishment and confidence in their abilities. By breaking down larger goals into smaller, more manageable tasks, individuals can set themselves up for success and build their self-esteem along the way. It is important to remember that even small achievements should be acknowledged and celebrated, as they contribute to a sense of self-worth. Practicing self-care is a crucial component of enhancing self-esteem. This involves taking care of one's physical, mental, and emotional well-being. Engaging in regular exercise, eating nutritious meals, and getting enough sleep can have a positive impact on self-esteem. Engaging in activities that bring joy and fulfillment, such as hobbies and interests, can boost self-esteem by providing a sense of purpose and accomplishment.

In addition to these strategies, seeking support from others is essential in enhancing self-esteem. Sur rounding oneself with positive and supportive individuals can help counteract feelings of insecurity and self-doubt. It is important to build a strong social network of friends and family members who uplift and encourage, as their validation and affirmations can contribute to an individual's sense of self-worth. Practicing self-compassion is crucial for enhancing self-esteem and overcoming insecurity. Individuals with low self-esteem are overly critical of themselves, setting impossibly high standards and punishing themselves for perceived failures. By practicing self-compassion, individuals can learn to treat themselves with kindness, understanding, and forgiveness. This involves acknowledging that everyone makes mistakes, embracing imperfections, and being gentle with oneself in times of difficulty or adversity. Enhancing self-esteem is vital for overcoming insecurity. By challenging negative self-talk, setting achievable goals, practicing self-care, seeking support, and practicing self-compassion, individuals can begin to develop a positive and healthy sense of self-worth. While enhancing self-esteem requires effort and consistency, the long-term benefits in terms of overcoming insecurity and leading a more fulfilling life are well worth it.

CHALLENGING NEGATIVE BELIEFS AND REPLACING THEM WITH POSITIVE AFFIRMATIONS

Negative beliefs can stem from a variety of sources, such as past failures, societal pressure, or even negative self-talk. These beliefs can manifest as self-doubt, fear of failure, or a lack of self-worth. In order to overcome insecurity, it is essential to recognize and challenge these negative beliefs. This can be done by questioning the evidence behind these beliefs and examining whether they are based on facts or simply assumptions. For example, if someone believes they are incapable of succeeding in their chosen career due to a past failure, they can challenge this belief by considering the lessons learned from that failure and acknowledging their current strengths and achievements. By challenging negative beliefs in this way, individuals can begin to build a more realistic perception of themselves and their abilities. Once negative beliefs have been challenged, it is important to replace them with positive affirmations. Positive affirmations are statements that reflect one's positive qualities, abilities, and potential. These affirmations help to counteract the negative beliefs and thoughts that contribute to insecurity. By consciously repeating positive affirmations, individuals can reprogram their minds to focus on their strengths and accomplishments rather than their weaknesses and failures. For instance, someone who struggles with body image issues can replace negative self-talk like "I am ugly" or "I will never be attractive" with positive affirmations like "I am beautiful just the way I am" or "I deserve to feel confident in my own skin". Over time, these positive affirmations can help to build self-confidence and cultivate a healthier self-image. In order for challenging negative beliefs and utilizing positive affirmations to be effective in overcoming insecurity, consistency and repetition are key. It is important to practice these techniques regularly and make them a part of one's daily routine. This might involve setting aside dedicated time each day for positive affirmations or incorporating them into existing routines, such as repeating affirmations while getting ready in the morning or before going to bed at night. By consistently challenging negative beliefs and reinforcing positive affirmations, individuals can gradually shift their mindset and develop a more secure sense of self. Overcoming insecurity requires the deliberate effort to challenge negative beliefs and replace them with positive affirmations. By recognizing and questioning negative beliefs, individuals can begin to build a more realistic perception of themselves and their abilities. By consistently practicing positive affirmations, individuals can recalibrate their minds to focus on their strengths and accomplishments. Through these efforts, insecurity can be gradually overcome, allowing individuals to embrace their worth and potential.

SETTING ACHIEVABLE GOALS TO BOOST CONFIDENCE

In addition to reframing negative self-talk, another effective strategy for overcoming insecurity is setting achievable goals to boost confidence. Goals provide a clear direction and sense of purpose, which can help individuals regain a sense of control and agency over their lives. When setting goals, it is important to make them realistic and attainable to prevent further feelings of failure or disappointment. By starting with small, manageable goals and gradually increasing their complexity and difficulty, individuals can build a foundation of success and accomplishment. The achievement of these goals serves as evidence of one's capabilities and strengths, leading to an increased sense of self-worth. Reaching goals provides a sense of satisfaction and fulfillment, which can further enhance self-confidence. One effective method for setting achievable goals is using the SMART framework. SMART stands for Specific, Measurable, Attainable, Relevant, and Time-bound. By following this framework, individuals can ensure that their goals are well-defined and structured in a way that facilitates success. For example, instead of setting a vague goal like "Improve my physical fitness," a SMART goal would be "Attend the gym three times a week for at least 30 minutes each, for the next three months." This goal is specific in terms of the frequency and duration of gym visits, measurable by tracking the number of workouts completed, attainable within the given timeframe and personal circumstances, relevant to improving physical fitness, and time-bound with a clear deadline of three months.

It is important to celebrate and acknowledge each milestone achieved on the path to reaching a goal. By recognizing and rewarding progress, individuals reinforce their belief in their own capabilities, further boosting their confidence. This can be done through small acts of self-care or by sharing achievements with others. Celebrating milestones not only provides a sense of validation but also motivates individuals to continue pursuing their goals and overcoming their insecurities.

Seeking support from others can greatly contribute to the process of setting achievable goals and building confidence. Surrounding oneself with a supportive network of friends, family, or mentors provides encouragement, accountability, and valuable feedback. Sharing goals with trusted individuals can generate a sense of shared responsibility and commitment, making the journey towards achievement more enjoyable and less daunting. Receiving guidance and advice from others who have already reached similar goals can provide valuable insights and strategies for success. Overcoming insecurity requires setting achievable goals that boost confidence. By using the SMART framework to set well-defined and measurable goals, individuals can regain a sense of control and success. Celebrating milestones along the way and seeking support from others further enhances confidence and motivation. With these strategies in place, individuals can gradually overcome their insecurities and embark on a journey of self-discovery and personal growth.

SURROUNDING ONESELF WITH SUPPORTIVE INDIVIDUALS

When individuals surround themselves with supportive individuals, they are more likely to feel accepted and valued, which can help to alleviate self-doubt and increase self-confidence. Having a support system in place can provide individuals with reassurance that they are not alone in their struggles and that there are people who care about their well-being. Friends and family members who offer encouragement, empathy, and understanding can play a crucial role in helping individuals develop a more positive self-image. They can serve as a sounding board for self-doubts and insecurities, providing valuable perspective and support. Supportive individuals can also act as role models, exhibiting traits and behaviors that promote self-confidence and self-assurance. By observing and interacting with these individuals, insecure individuals can learn new ways of thinking and behaving that can contribute to their personal growth and development. Surrounding oneself with supportive individuals can also help to create a positive social environment where individuals feel safe and comfortable expressing themselves without fear of judgment or rejection. This supportive social network can provide opportunities for personal and social development, allowing individuals to engage in activities and relationships that foster their self-esteem and self-worth. For example, participating in group activities or joining support groups can offer a sense of belonging and camaraderie, which can help to counteract insecurities and build self-confidence. Supportive individuals can provide feedback and constructive criticism in a caring and nurturing manner. This feedback can help individuals identify areas for improvement and growth without feeling attacked or invalidated. Having supportive individuals in their lives can also serve as a buffer against negative influences and toxic relationships. By surrounding themselves with people who prioritize their well-being, individuals can distance themselves from those who may perpetuate their insecurities or contribute to their self-doubts. The support and encouragement provided by these individuals can create a more positive and nurturing environment, facilitating personal growth and self-acceptance. Although insecurity can be a challenging emotion to overcome, there are several strategies that individuals can employ to foster self-confidence and self-assurance. Challenging negative thoughts and beliefs, practicing self-compassion, and surrounding oneself with supportive individuals are all effective ways to mitigate insecurities. By implementing these strategies, individuals can cultivate a more positive self-image, develop resilience, and ultimately overcome their insecurities. While the journey may not be easy, with determination and persistence, individuals can emerge from their insecurities stronger, more confident, and more self-assured. Overcoming insecurity requires a multifaceted approach that includes self-reflection, building self-esteem, and seeking support. Self-reflection entails understanding the root causes of insecurity, such as past traumas or negative experiences, and working towards healing and growth. This can be done through therapy, journaling, or engaging in activities that promote self-awareness, such as meditation or Mindfulness practices. Building self-esteem involves recognizing and challenging negative self-talk, setting realistic goals, and celebrating personal achievements. Developing self-compassion and embracing one's uniqueness are also crucial components of enhancing self-esteem. Seeking support from trusted friends, family members, or even professionals can provide invaluable guidance and encouragement during the journey towards overcoming insecurity. Engaging in meaningful connections and relationships can also increase feelings of validation, belonging, and self-worth. Engaging in self-care activities, such as regular exercise, adequate sleep, and a balanced diet, can contribute to overall well-being and help combat feelings of insecurity. It is important to recognize that overcoming insecurity is a process that takes time and effort. It requires a willingness to confront fears, challenge societal expectations, and prioritize self-care. By embracing vulnerability and practicing self-compassion, individuals can gradually dismantle the barriers that insecurity creates and foster a sense of worthiness and belonging. While insecurity may always be present to some degree, learning to manage and overcome it can lead to a more fulfilling and authentic life. As individuals, we have the power to reshape our internal narratives and cultivate a sense of self that is rooted in self-acceptance and resilience. Though the journey may be challenging at times, the rewards of overcoming insecurity far outweigh the temporary discomfort. By embracing our imperfections, taking risks, and surrounding ourselves with a supportive network, we can break free from the grips of insecurity and live a life that is guided by self-love, confidence, and fulfillment. The key lies within our willingness to embark on this transformative journey and commit to our personal growth. Regardless of where we are on this path, it is never too late to take the first step and start cultivating the life we deserve.

V. ADOPTING A GROWTH MINDSET

A growth mindset is the belief that one's abilities and intelligence can be developed through dedication and hard work. This mindset views setbacks and challenges as opportunities for learning and growth, rather than as indications of inherent flaws or limitations. When individuals with a growth mindset encounter obstacles, they approach them with resilience and determination, knowing that effort and perseverance are key to achieving success. This mindset enables individuals to embrace their imperfections and mistakes as valuable lessons and steppingstones toward self-improvement. The first step in adopting a growth mindset is recognizing and challenging fixed beliefs about oneself. Individuals with insecurity often hold fixed beliefs about their abilities, talents, and worth, which are deeply ingrained and difficult to change. By becoming aware of these beliefs and questioning their validity, individuals can open themselves up to new possibilities and growth. For example, instead of believing that they are inherently bad at public speaking, individuals can reframe their thinking and acknowledge that public speaking skills can be developed with practice and effort. Another important aspect of developing a growth mindset is reframing failures as learning opportunities. Insecurity often leads individuals to perceive failures as personal shortcomings, which can hinder their willingness to take risks and try new things. By embracing failures as steppingstones to success, individuals can cultivate resilience and perseverance. They can view setbacks as valuable feedback that helps them improve and refine their skills. This shift in perspective enables individuals to approach challenges with a sense of curiosity and a willingness to try again, rather than succumbing to self-doubt and avoiding future opportunities. Adopting a growth mindset involves seeking and accepting feedback from others. Insecurity often stems from a fear of being judged or criticized by others. Feedback can be an instrumental tool for growth and self-improvement. By actively seeking feedback, individuals can gain valuable insights into their strengths and weaknesses, enabling them to make targeted efforts to improve. Accepting feedback with an open mind and a willingness to learn demonstrates a growth-oriented attitude. It shows that individuals recognize the value of constructive criticism and are committed to personal growth and development. Developing a growth mindset requires embracing the process of learning and cultivating a passion for continuous improvement. Insecurity often leads individuals to focus solely on the end result, fixating on perfection and comparing themselves to others. Adopting a growth mindset entails valuing and embracing the journey of learning and growth. It involves maintaining a sense of curiosity, celebrating progress, and viewing challenges as opportunities for further development. This mindset shift fosters a positive and empowering attitude toward personal growth, enabling individuals to overcome insecurities and reach their full potential. Adopting a growth mindset is a crucial step in overcoming insecurity. By challenging fixed beliefs, reframing failures, seeking feedback, and embracing the learning process, individuals can cultivate resilience, perseverance, and a sense of self-worth. Developing a growth mindset is not an overnight process but rather an ongoing commitment to personal growth and improvement. With time and effort, individuals can overcome their insecurities and embrace their strengths, enabling them to navigate the challenges of life with confidence and optimism.

UNDERSTANDING THE CONCEPT OF A GROWTH MINDSET

A growth mindset is the belief that intelligence and abilities can be developed through dedication and hard work, rather than being fixed traits. This mindset acknowledges that individuals have the potential to grow, change, and improve their skills and talents. In contrast, a fixed mindset is the belief that intelligence and abilities are set in stone, leading individuals to fear failure and avoid challenges. Embracing a growth mindset can empower individuals to face their insecurities head-on, as they recognize that setbacks and failures are not indicative of their worth or abilities. Instead, they view them as opportunities for learning and growth. This mindset encourages individuals to see obstacles and setbacks as temporary roadblocks that can be overcome with effort and perseverance. By understanding the concept of a growth mindset, individuals can shift their focus from seeking validation and approval to striving for personal growth and achievement. They become more motivated to take on challenges and view them as opportunities to develop new skills and improve existing ones. A growth mindset also fosters resilience, as individuals understand that setbacks are a normal part of the learning process and do not define their abilities or potential. This attitude helps individuals overcome insecurity by reframing their negative self-perceptions and embracing a more positive and growth-oriented outlook. A growth mindset encourages individuals to seek feedback and constructive criticism as valuable tools for improvement. Instead of feeling threatened or defensive, they welcome opportunities to learn from others and use feedback as a means of further developing their skills and knowledge. This mindset also promotes self-reflection, as individuals actively analyze their past performance and identify areas for improvement. They understand that growth does not happen overnight and that progress often requires patience, dedication, and resilience. Understanding the concept of a growth mindset also helps individuals cultivate a sense of purpose and meaning in their pursuits. They recognize that personal growth and development are lifelong journeys, rather than finite goals. This mindset encourages them to set ambitious yet realistic goals, approach challenges with a positive attitude, and persevere in the face of adversity. A growth mindset fosters a sense of self-belief and confidence. Individuals who possess this mindset understand that their capabilities and intelligence are not fixed, but rather malleable and expandable. This belief in their ability to improve gives them the confidence to take risks, push beyond their comfort zones, and seize opportunities for growth and achievement. Understanding the concept of a growth mindset is crucial for overcoming insecurity. By adopting this mindset, individuals can transform their negative self-perceptions, view setbacks as opportunities for learning and growth, seek feedback and constructive criticism, cultivate resilience, purpose, and confidence, and, most importantly, take control of their own personal development and achievement.

EMBRACING FAILURES AS OPPORTUNITIES FOR GROWTH

Failure is often seen as a negative outcome, leading to feelings of disappointment, shame, and self-doubt. By reframing failures as opportunities for growth, individuals can break free from the cycle of insecurity and develop a more positive perspective. Embracing failures requires a shift in mindset, allowing individuals to see setbacks as valuable learning experiences rather than personal shortcomings. When faced with failure, individuals should ask themselves what they can learn from the experience and how they can use it to improve. This mindset shift allows individuals to focus on their personal growth rather than dwelling on their insecurities. Failure also provides individuals with the opportunity to develop resilience and perseverance. By embracing failures and learning from them, individuals can gain the strength to overcome future challenges and setbacks. Insecure individuals often fear failure because they believe it confirms their underlying insecurities. By embracing failures as opportunities for growth, individuals can break free from this limiting belief and realize that failure is not a reflection of their worth or capabilities. Instead, failure should be seen as a natural part of the learning process. It is through failure that individuals can refine their skills, develop new strategies, and ultimately achieve success. Embracing failures also requires individuals to let go of perfectionism. Many individuals struggling with insecurity strive for perfection as a means of avoiding failure and criticism. This perfectionistic mindset puts immense pressure on individuals and can further fuel feelings of insecurity. By embracing failures, individuals can let go of the need for perfection and instead focus on progress and personal growth. Perfectionism is not sustainable, and individuals who constantly strive for perfection are more likely to experience burnout and increased levels of insecurity. Embracing failures also involves practicing self-compassion. Instead of harshly judging oneself for failure, individuals should practice kindness and understanding. Failure is an inevitable part of life, and berating oneself for mistakes only serves to heighten feelings of insecurity. By offering oneself compassion and understanding, individuals can develop a healthier relationship with failure, allowing for personal growth and increased self-confidence. Embracing failures as opportunities for growth is a fundamental step in overcoming insecurities. By reframing failures as valuable learning experiences, individuals can break free from the cycle of insecurity and develop a more positive perspective. This involves shifting one's mindset, letting go of perfectionism, and practicing self-compassion. Failure is not a reflection of one's worth or capabilities, but rather a steppingstone towards personal growth and success. By embracing failures and learning from them, individuals can develop resilience, perseverance, and ultimately overcome their insecurities.

FOSTERING A DESIRE TO LEARN AND IMPROVE CONSTANTLY

Insecurity often stems from a lack of confidence in one's abilities or a fear of failure. By cultivating a hunger for knowledge and personal growth, individuals can combat these feelings of insecurity and develop a sense of self-assurance. One method to foster this desire is through the pursuit of education. Engaging in higher education, such as attending college, can provide individuals with the tools and resources necessary to expand their knowledge base and acquire new skills. By immersing oneself in an academic environment, surrounded by like-minded peers and experienced educators, one can gain a sense of purpose and motivation to succeed. Higher education offers opportunities for personal discovery and self-improvement, enabling individuals to explore their interests and passions, ultimately building confidence in their abilities. The desire to learn can extend beyond formal education, as individuals can also seek out alternative avenues for personal growth. This can manifest in various forms, such as attending workshops, seminars, or conferences related to their area of interest. By participating in such events, individuals can engage with experts in their field, learn from their experiences, and enhance their knowledge and skills. The advent of technology has made learning more accessible than ever before. Online platforms and resources provide individuals with the opportunity to learn at their own pace and explore new subjects independently. Adopting a continuous learning mindset allows individuals to overcome insecurity by acknowledging that knowledge is not fixed, but rather something that can be built upon and expanded. Alongside the pursuit of education, another effective strategy for fostering a desire to learn and improve constantly is by seeking out constructive feedback. Insecurity arises from a fear of judgment or criticism. Viewing feedback as an opportunity for growth rather than a personal attack can transform insecurity into an engine for improvement. By actively seeking feedback from trusted individuals, such as mentors or peers, individuals can gain valuable insights into their strengths and areas for development. This feedback allows individuals to identify specific areas of improvement, set goals, and work towards personal growth. Seeking feedback can also provide a sense of validation and recognition, further bolstering individuals' self-confidence. Fostering a desire for constant improvement requires maintaining a growth mindset. Embracing the belief that abilities can be developed through dedication and hard work, rather than being fixed traits, allows individuals to approach challenges with a positive attitude and resilience. By reframing setbacks as opportunities for learning and improvement, individuals can overcome feelings of insecurity and maintain a sense of motivation and perseverance. Fostering a desire to learn and improve constantly is crucial in overcoming insecurity. Engaging in higher education, seeking out alternative avenues for growth, actively seeking feedback, and maintaining a growth mindset all contribute to building self-assurance and confidence.

By cultivating a hunger for knowledge, individuals can transform their insecurities into opportunities for personal growth and achievement. In addition to the aforementioned strategies, cultivating self-compassion is vital in overcoming insecurity.

Self-compassion is the practice of treating oneself with kindness, understanding, and acceptance during times of struggle or difficulty. Research has shown that individuals who are self-compassionate are better able to cope with insecurities and experience greater levels of well-being.

One way to cultivate self-compassion is through the practice of Mindfulness. Mindfulness involves being fully present in the moment and nonjudgmentally observing one's thoughts and feelings. By practicing Mindfulness, individuals can become more aware of their insecurities and the negative self-talk that often accompanies them. By learning to observe these thoughts and feelings without judgment, individuals can develop a more compassionate and understanding attitude toward themselves.

Another way to cultivate self-compassion is by practicing self-care. Taking care of oneself is essential for overall well-being and can help to counteract feelings of insecurity. Engaging in activities that bring joy and relaxation, such as exercise, spending time with loved ones, or engaging in hobbies, can boost self-esteem and confidence. Practicing self-care involves setting boundaries and prioritizing one's needs, which can promote a sense of self-worth and security. In addition to self-compassion, developing a growth mindset is crucial in overcoming insecurity. A growth mindset is the belief that intelligence and abilities can be developed through effort and practice. Individuals with a growth mindset are more likely to view setbacks and challenges as opportunities for growth, rather than as indicators of their inherent worth or abilities. By cultivating a growth mindset, individuals can reframe their insecurities as opportunities for personal development and learning.

One way to develop a growth mindset is by reframing negative self-talk. Insecurities often manifest in harsh and critical self-talk, which can reinforce feelings of inadequacy. By consciously replacing negative self-talk with more positive and encouraging thoughts, individuals can begin to shift their mindset and build confidence. Seeking support from others is crucial in overcoming insecurity. Building a strong support network of friends, family, or mentors can provide individuals with the reassurance and validation they need to combat feelings of insecurity. Opening up to trusted individuals about one's insecurities can also help to challenge and reframe negative beliefs. Seeking professional help, such as therapy or counseling, can provide individuals with the tools and strategies needed to address and overcome deep-seated insecurities. Overcoming insecurity requires a multi-faceted approach. By exploring the underlying causes of insecurity, challenging negative beliefs and thought patterns, cultivating self-compassion and a growth mindset, and seeking support, individuals can begin to break free from the grips of insecurity and cultivate stronger self-esteem and confidence. Although the journey may be challenging at times, the rewards of increased self-acceptance and resilience are well worth the effort.

VI. BUILDING RESILIENCE

Resilience is the ability to bounce back from difficult situations or setbacks, and it plays a crucial role in our overall mental well-being. There are several strategies individuals can use to cultivate resilience and develop a strong sense of self-assurance. First and foremost, it is important to foster a positive mindset. This involves reframing negative thoughts and focusing on one's strengths and accomplishments rather than dwelling on perceived failures or shortcomings. By consciously redirecting our thoughts to more positive aspects of our lives, we can gradually shift our mindset from one of self-doubt to one of self-assurance. Connecting with supportive and nurturing relationships is instrumental in building resilience. Surrounding oneself with individuals who truly believe in our capabilities and provide a safe space for vulnerability fosters a sense of belonging and strengthens our self-confidence. These relationships serve as a source of reassurance and encouragement, helping us navigate through times of insecurity. Another strategy to build resilience is to set and pursue achievable goals. By breaking down larger aspirations into manageable steps, we can experience a sense of accomplishment, which boosts our self-esteem and cultivates resilience. Developing and maintaining healthy habits is integral to building resilience. This includes practicing self-care activities such as exercise, meditation, and pursuing hobbies or interests that bring us joy. Taking care of our physical and mental well-being replenishes our energy and equips us with the strength to face challenges head-on. It is important to cultivate a growth mindset. Embracing a belief that we can learn and improve from failures or setbacks rather than seeing them as permanent obstacles enhances our resilience. This shift in perspective allows us to view challenges as opportunities for growth and development. Seeking professional help such as therapy or counseling can provide valuable tools and techniques to overcome insecurity. A trained therapist can help individuals identify underlying insecurities and develop strategies to overcome them, offering a safe and confidential space for self-reflection and personal growth. It is essential to practice self-compassion throughout this journey. Recognizing that insecurity is a natural human emotion and offering ourselves kindness and understanding when we experience it is vital. Being gentle with ourselves during periods of self-doubt allows us to build resilience and develop a stronger sense of self-assurance over time. In sum, building resilience is a multifaceted process that requires a commitment to personal growth and self-reflection. By fostering a positive mindset, connecting with supportive relationships, setting achievable goals, engaging in healthy habits, embracing a growth mindset, seeking professional help, and practicing self-compassion, individuals can cultivate resilience and overcome insecurity. It is important to recognize that building resilience is a lifelong journey and that setbacks are a natural part of growth. By continuously applying these strategies and learning from every challenge, individuals can develop a strong foundation of self-assurance and navigate through life with greater confidence and resilience.

DEVELOPING COPING MECHANISMS TO DEAL WITH SETBACKS

Setbacks are a natural part of life, and without the ability to cope with them effectively, they can amplify feelings of insecurity. One effective coping mechanism is reframing setbacks as opportunities for growth. Rather than viewing a setback as a personal failure, reframing it as a chance to learn and improve can help individuals maintain a positive mindset. Another coping mechanism is to focus on what can be controlled. Setbacks are caused by external factors beyond one's control, and dwelling on these aspects can be counterproductive. By accepting what cannot be changed and shifting focus towards what can be controlled, individuals can regain a sense of agency and reduce feelings of helplessness. Seeking support from others is another important coping mechanism. Connecting with friends, family, or professionals who can provide guidance and encouragement can be immensely helpful in navigating setbacks. By sharing experiences and gaining a different perspective, individuals can gain new strategies and insights on how to approach and overcome setbacks. Engaging in self-care activities is also crucial in developing coping mechanisms. Taking care of physical, mental, and emotional well-being can provide a sense of stability and resilience in the face of setbacks. Engaging in activities such as exercise, Mindfulness, and hobbies can help individuals maintain a sense of balance and self-worth. Setting realistic goals and expectations is essential in developing coping mechanisms. Unrealistic expectations can perpetuate feelings of insecurity and disappointment. By setting achievable and realistic goals, individuals can celebrate small successes and build confidence over time. Developing coping mechanisms is an ongoing process that requires self-reflection and practice. It is important to remember that setbacks are temporary and do not define one's worth or potential. By reframing setbacks, focusing on what can be controlled, seeking support, engaging in self-care activities, and setting realistic goals, individuals can overcome insecurity and emerge stronger and more resilient. Coping mechanisms provide individuals with the necessary tools and strategies to navigate setbacks in a healthy and productive way. Through the development of these skills, individuals can become more equipped to deal with adversity and setbacks, ultimately leading to personal growth and increased self-confidence. With practice and perseverance, individuals can learn to view setbacks as opportunities for growth and cultivate a resilient mindset. Overcoming insecurity is a journey, and developing effective coping mechanisms is an integral part of that journey. By acknowledging setbacks as normal and temporary, individuals can embrace the challenges they face and work towards overcoming them. In turn, this can lead to a greater sense of self-worth, inner strength, and a more positive outlook on life.

PRACTICING SELF-COMPASSION AND FORGIVENESS

In addition to challenging negative thoughts and seeking support from others, practicing self-compassion and forgiveness is crucial in overcoming insecurity. Self-compassion involves treating oneself with kindness and understanding, rather than being overly critical or judgmental. It requires acknowledging that nobody is perfect and that making mistakes is a part of being human. Forgiving oneself for these mistakes is equally important, as holding onto guilt or shame only reinforces feelings of insecurity. By practicing self-compassion and forgiveness, individuals can break free from the vicious cycle of self-doubt and build a healthier and more secure sense of self.

Self-compassion is the antidote to the harsh self-criticism that often accompanies insecurity. When individuals embrace self-compassion, they acknowledge their own suffering and respond with kindness and understanding, just as they would to a close friend. This entails reframing negative self-talk into more compassionate and realistic statements. For example, instead of berating oneself for a perceived failure, one can remind oneself that mistakes happen and that it is an opportunity for growth and learning. By adopting this compassionate mindset, individuals can begin to see themselves in a more positive light and develop a greater sense of self-worth.

Practicing forgiveness is an essential step in overcoming insecurity. Individuals hold onto past mistakes or shortcomings, allowing them to define their sense of self. These self-imposed labels and judgments only serve to perpetuate feelings of insecurity. Forgiveness involves letting go of these negative beliefs and allowing oneself to move forward. It is important to recognize that everyone makes mistakes and that these mistakes do not define one's worth as a person. By forgiving oneself, individuals can release the burden of guilt and shame, and begin the process of healing and self-acceptance.

In addition, self-compassion and forgiveness serve as powerful tools for combatting the comparisons that fuel insecurity. In a society driven by social media highlight reels and constant self-evaluation, it is easy to fall into the trap of comparing oneself to others. This comparison often leads to feelings of inadequacy and doubt. By practicing self-compassion and forgiveness, individuals can learn to accept themselves for who they are, rather than striving to meet unrealistic standards set by others. By acknowledging their own strengths and unique qualities, individuals can distance themselves from the harmful cycle of comparison, fostering a stronger sense of self and a greater level of self-security. Practicing self-compassion and forgiveness is a fundamental aspect of overcoming insecurity. By treating oneself with kindness and understanding, individuals can break free from the grip of negative self-talk and develop a healthier self-image. Forgiveness allows individuals to let go of the past and embrace the present, enabling them to move forward with a sense of self-acceptance and growth. Together, self-compassion and forgiveness empower individuals to counteract comparison and build a stronger foundation of self-security.

LEARNING FROM PAST EXPERIENCES TO BOUNCE BACK STRONGER

Reflecting on previous encounters with insecurities allows individuals to gain valuable insights into their strengths and weaknesses, enabling them to develop a stronger sense of self. By analyzing past experiences, individuals can identify the triggers that contribute to their feelings of insecurity and develop strategies to avoid or overcome them in the future. The lessons learned from past insecurities can serve as a source of resilience, as individuals can draw upon their previous successes in overcoming adversity to face current challenges. One example of this is the story of JK Rowling, the renowned author of the Harry Potter series. Before achieving global success, Rowling experienced multiple rejections from publishers and faced financial difficulties as a single mother. She used these experiences as fuel to persevere, eventually becoming one of the most successful authors in history. Rowling's ability to learn from her past hardships allowed her to bounce back stronger and transformed her insecurities into sources of motivation and determination. Similarly, individuals can apply this approach by examining their past insecurities and using them as steppingstones towards personal growth. Another strategy that can be employed is seeking support from others who have overcome similar challenges. By connecting with individuals who have successfully navigated their own insecurities, individuals can gain valuable insights and guidance, fostering a sense of community and providing reassurance that they are not alone in their struggles. In addition to seeking support from others, individuals can also engage in self-reflection and introspection to gain a deeper understanding of their insecurities. This can be achieved through journaling, therapy, or simply taking the time to reflect on one's thoughts and emotions. By exploring the root causes of their insecurities, individuals can uncover underlying beliefs and patterns that contribute to these feelings. Armed with this awareness, they can challenge and reframe these negative beliefs, ultimately building a stronger sense of self-worth and confidence. Engaging in activities that promote self-care and self-compassion is crucial in the process of bouncing back stronger. Taking the time to prioritize one's well-being and engage in activities that bring joy and fulfillment can help individuals replenish their emotional reserves and develop a positive mindset. Activities such as exercise, meditation, and pursuing hobbies not only offer a sense of relaxation but also boost self-esteem and combat feelings of insecurity. Engaging in positive self-talk and challenging negative self-perceptions is vital in overcoming insecurity. By consciously replacing self-critical thoughts with affirming and empowering beliefs, individuals can slowly rewire their mindset and build a stronger foundation of self-confidence. Learning from past experiences to bounce back stronger requires individuals to adopt a growth mindset and view setbacks as opportunities for growth and self-improvement. By embracing challenges and utilizing the lessons learned from past insecurities, individuals can develop resilience, reinforce their self-worth, and overcome their insecurity to lead happier and more fulfilling lives.

It is important to develop a strong sense of self-worth in order to overcome insecurity. Insecurity often stems from a lack of confidence and belief in oneself. It is crucial to cultivate self-worth by recognizing and embracing one's strengths, talents, and unique qualities. This can be accomplished through positive affirmations and self-reflection. By acknowledging one's accomplishments and valuing oneself, individuals can begin to shift their mindset from one of self-doubt to one of self-assurance. Seeking support from others can be instrumental in overcoming insecurity. Surrounding oneself with supportive and encouraging individuals can help boost self-esteem and provide a strong support system. Whether it be seeking guidance from a trusted mentor or confiding in a close friend, having someone to lean on and confide in can make a world of difference. Support groups or therapy sessions can provide a safe space for individuals to share their insecurities and receive feedback and advice from others who may be going through similar struggles.

Another effective strategy for overcoming insecurity is to challenge and reframe negative thoughts. Insecurity often stems from distorted or negative self-perceptions. By consciously challenging these thoughts and replacing them with more realistic and positive ones, individuals can begin to break free from the cycle of insecurity. This can be done through practices such as cognitive-behavioral therapy, where individuals learn to recognize and reframe their negative thoughts.

Taking action and stepping out of one's comfort zone can help build confidence and alleviate insecurity. Insecurity holds individuals back from pursuing their goals and dreams. By pushing through fear and tackling new challenges, individuals can prove to themselves that they are capable and competent. This can be as simple as trying a new hobby, taking on a leadership role, or enrolling in a challenging course. Each small victory can serve as a steppingstone towards overcoming insecurity and embracing personal growth. Practicing self-compassion is essential in the journey to overcoming insecurity. Insecurity often leads to self-criticism and harsh judgment. By cultivating self-compassion and treating oneself with kindness and understanding, individuals can begin to break free from the cycle of negative self-talk and self-doubt. This can be achieved through Mindfulness practice, where individuals learn to observe their thoughts and emotions without judgment. Engaging in self-care activities such as exercise, meditation, and hobbies can help promote self-compassion and overall well-being.

Overcoming insecurity is a process that requires both self-reflection and action. By developing a strong sense of self-worth, seeking support from others, challenging negative thoughts, taking action, and practicing self-compassion, individuals can begin to break free from the chains of insecurity and embrace a more confident and fulfilling life. While the journey may be challenging at times, it is important to remember that everyone is deserving of self-acceptance and love. It is through overcoming insecurity that individuals can unlock their full potential and live a life filled with confidence and joy.

VII. CULTIVATING HEALTHY RELATIONSHIPS

In addition to working on individual self-esteem and self-worth, cultivating healthy relationships is another crucial aspect of overcoming insecurity. Healthy relationships not only provide a source of support and encouragement but also offer an opportunity for personal growth and self-reflection. One key factor in cultivating healthy relationships is setting boundaries. Boundaries help individuals establish their personal limits and define what is acceptable and unacceptable within their relationships. By clearly communicating their needs and expectations, individuals can create an environment that promotes mutual respect and understanding. Healthy relationships require effective communication. It is essential to express oneself honestly and assertively, while also listening actively and empathetically to others. Effective communication fosters emotional intimacy and validates one's feelings and experiences. Developing trust is fundamental to building healthy relationships. Trust is built over time through consistent actions, openness, and honesty. It involves showing reliability, dependability, and a genuine concern for the well-being of the other person. Trust also includes believing in the other person's capabilities, which enhances their sense of self-worth. Healthy relationships require boundaries when it comes to conflicts and disagreements. Instead of avoiding or suppressing conflicts, healthy relationships encourage open discussions where both parties can express their opinions and concerns.

This allows for problem-solving and compromise, leading to greater understanding and harmony. It is crucial to approach conflicts with empathy and a willingness to understand the other person's perspective. Self-care plays a significant role in cultivating healthy relationships. Nurturing oneself physically, emotionally, and mentally allows individuals to show up authentically in their relationships. Taking care of oneself includes developing one's interests, hobbies, and passions, as well as setting aside time for relaxation and self-reflection. When individuals prioritize self-care, they can contribute positively to their relationships without feeling overwhelmed or depleted.

Overcoming insecurity is a challenging journey that requires self-reflection, self-com passion, and intentional efforts. By understanding the roots of insecurity and recognizing the negative thought patterns that contribute to it, individuals can work towards building a positive self-image. Developing a growth mindset, practicing self-compassion, and surrounding oneself with a supportive community can foster resilience and inner strength. Cultivating healthy relationships is crucial in overcoming insecurity. Setting boundaries, practicing effective communication, building trust, and approaching conflicts with empathy are vital in creating relationships that promote personal growth and self-worth. Prioritizing self-care plays a significant role in maintaining healthy relationships and contributing positively to them. With dedication and perseverance, individuals can overcome their insecurities and lead fulfilling and confident lives. It is through transformation and growth that individuals can foster a sense of self-worth and authenticity, allowing them to thrive in all areas of their lives.

NURTURING MEANINGFUL CONNECTIONS WITH OTHERS

In addition to cultivating self-acceptance as a means of overcoming insecurities, nurturing meaningful connections with others plays a crucial role in this process. Genuine connections with individuals who understand, support, and believe in our abilities can foster a sense of belonging and worthiness, relieving us from feelings of insecurity. One way to nurture these connections is through effective communication. It is essential to be an active listener, truly engaging with others and demonstrating genuine interest in their thoughts, feelings, and experiences. By validating their emotions and actively empathizing, we can create a safe and nurturing space for authentic connections to form. Practicing vulnerability with trustworthy individuals can create stronger bonds and deeper connections. Sharing our insecurities, fears, and vulnerabilities with others allows us to be seen and understood, fostering a sense of acceptance and validation. This process requires courage and trust, but the rewards can be transformative. Building a support system comprised of non-judgmental and compassionate individuals can provide emotional reassurance during challenging times, reminding us that we are not alone in our struggles. Nurturing meaningful connections with others involves investing time and effort into maintaining and deepening these relationships. This can be achieved through regular communication, planning activities together, and demonstrating care and support for one another. By consistently showing up for others and being present in their lives, we can strengthen the bonds that connect us, creating a web of support that helps alleviate feelings of insecurity. Engaging in shared experiences and collaborating on meaningful projects can foster a sense of belonging and purpose, reminding us of our inherent value and abilities. Supporting others in their endeavors can also contribute to our own sense of self-worth and confidence. By celebrating the successes and achievements of those in our lives, we reinforce the belief that we too are capable of growth and accomplishments. This reciprocal support system creates a positive feedback loop, boosting our self-image and reducing insecurities in the process. Nurturing meaningful connections with others is a transformative and essential component of overcoming insecurity. Through effective communication, practicing vulnerability, and investing in our relationships, we create a stronghold against self-doubt and negativity. Meaningful connections provide us with a sense of belonging and validation, reminding us that our worth is not determined by our insecurities. By surrounding ourselves with individuals who believe in our abilities and support our personal growth, we cultivate an environment that empowers us to overcome our insecurities and embrace our true potential. These connections serve as a source of encouragement and inspiration during challenging times, reminding us that we are not alone in our struggles. As we continue to nurture meaningful connections with others, we not only strengthen our own sense of self-worth but also contribute to a more compassionate and supportive community, encouraging others to do the same.

COMMUNICATING ASSERTIVELY AND SETTING BOUNDARIES

When individuals struggle with insecurities, they often lack the confidence to express themselves assertively and establish healthy boundaries. Developing assertive communication skills is crucial in expressing thoughts, feelings, and opinions in a respectful and confident manner. It involves effective listening and expressing oneself without being aggressive or passive. As stated by Nelson-Jones (2017), assertive communication allows individuals to have their needs met while considering the needs of others, promoting healthy relationships and minimizing conflicts. Setting boundaries plays a vital role in overcoming insecurity as it establishes limits and protects one's emotional and physical well-being. By setting boundaries, individuals create a sense of control and demonstrate self-respect, which ultimately boosts self-confidence. According to Cloud and Townsend (2017), establishing boundaries involves communicating them clearly and consistently, considering personal needs and values, and effectively managing relationships. Effective communication and boundary-setting require practice and self-reflection. Developing assertiveness can often involve learning how to say "no" when necessary, advocating for personal needs, and expressing emotions constructively. These skills can be further refined through various techniques such as active listening, using "I" statements, and body language awareness. In addition to assertive communication, setting boundaries requires individuals to identify their limits and communicate them to others.

This involves recognizing when personal values and needs are being compromised and taking steps to rectify the situation. By doing so, individuals assert their right to be treated with dignity and respect, fostering a sense of security and well-being. It is important to note that assertiveness and boundary-setting should be balanced with empathy and consideration for others. While it is essential to advocate for personal needs, it is equally crucial to acknowledge and respect the needs of others. Building assertive communication skills and establishing boundaries can collectively contribute to overcoming insecurity by creating a foundation of self-assurance and resilience. Insecurity often stems from a fear of rejection, disapproval, or judgment. By effectively expressing oneself and setting boundaries, individuals develop the self-confidence to withstand potential criticism or rejection, reducing feelings of insecurity. Assertive communication and boundary-setting can lead to healthier relationships as individuals are able to advocate for their needs and establish mutual respect. This allows for better communication, increased trust, and enhanced emotional well-being. Overcoming insecurity is a journey that requires self-reflection and active practice. By honing assertive communication skills and setting boundaries, individuals can transform their perceptions of themselves and their relationships. As individuals develop their assertiveness, they become more in tune with their needs and assert their right to establish boundaries that align with their values. This not only empowers them to advocate for themselves but also cultivates a sense of self-worth and security. The development of assertive communication and boundary-setting skills provides individuals with the tools to overcome insecurity and foster healthy relationships with themselves and others.

BEING OPEN TO FEEDBACK AND CONSTRUCTIVE CRITICISM

One of the main reasons for insecurity is the fear of judgment and the need for approval from others. By being open to feedback and constructive criticism, individuals can gain valuable insights and perspectives that can help them grow and improve. It requires a willingness to listen, reflect, and consider alternative viewpoints, even if they might be challenging or uncomfortable to hear. Embracing feedback can be a transformative experience as it allows individuals to understand their strengths and weaknesses objectively. Feedback and constructive criticism can serve as sources of motivation and encouragement. It provides individuals with the opportunity to learn from their mistakes and enhance their performance. In the face of insecurity, it can be tempting to avoid feedback altogether, fearing that it will only confirm one's self-doubts and shortcomings. By actively seeking feedback, individuals demonstrate a willingness to confront their insecurities head-on, fostering personal growth and resilience. Constructive criticism can also serve as a reality check, helping individuals gain a more accurate perception of themselves and their abilities. Being open to feedback and constructive criticism also fosters effective communication and interpersonal relationships. When individuals openly receive feedback, whether it be positive or critical, it shows a level of respect and trust for others' opinions and perspectives. In turn, this encourages others to engage in honest and open conversations, allowing for the exchange of ideas and constructive dialogue. By actively seeking feedback and acknowledging areas for improvement, individuals signal their commitment to personal and professional development, creating an environment of growth and collaboration. Being open to feedback also requires discernment. Not all feedback is constructive or helpful. It is essential to critically evaluate the source and intention behind the feedback received. Constructive criticism should focus on addressing specific behaviors or actions rather than attacking one's character. Individuals should differentiate between subjective opinions and valid feedback based on expertise and experience. It is crucial not to let unwarranted criticism or negative opinions undermine one's self-worth or discourage personal growth. Being open to feedback and constructive criticism is a crucial step in overcoming insecurity. It requires individuals to embrace vulnerability, acknowledge their weaknesses, and actively seek opportunities for growth. By valuing feedback, individuals can gain valuable insights, enhance their performance, and build stronger relationships. It is essential to approach feedback with discernment, evaluating its source and intention to filter out unhelpful criticism. Through this process, individuals can gradually overcome their insecurities, develop resilience, and foster personal and professional growth.

One effective way to overcome insecurity is to cultivate self-compassion. Self-compassion involves treating oneself with kindness, understanding, and acceptance, especially in times of difficulty or failure. It is about recognizing that no one is perfect and that making mistakes is a natural part of being human. Many individuals struggle with insecurity because they hold themselves to impossibly high standards and are overly critical of their own flaws and shortcomings. By practicing self-compassion, individuals can learn to be kinder and more understanding towards themselves, which can help to reduce feelings of insecurity. Research has shown that practicing self-compassion has numerous psychological benefits. For instance, a study conducted by Neff and Vonk (2009) found that individuals who scored higher in self-compassion reported lower levels of social anxiety and fear of negative evaluation. This suggests that self-compassion may be particularly effective in alleviating insecurity in social situations. Self-compassion has been found to increase self-esteem and self-worth, which are essential components of overcoming insecurity. By practicing self-compassion, individuals can learn to recognize their own inherent value and worth, regardless of their flaws or failures. It allows individuals to develop a more realistic and balanced view of themselves, rather than focusing solely on their perceived shortcomings. Self-compassion can help individuals to develop a sense of resilience and bounce back from setbacks or failures. When individuals are kind and understanding towards themselves, they are more likely to view failures or mistakes as opportunities for growth and learning, rather than as indications of their inherent worth or abilities. This mindset shift can be transformative in overcoming insecurity, as individuals begin to see themselves as capable and resilient, rather than flawed or inadequate. Practicing self-compassion involves a number of strategies. One common technique is to practice self-talk or inner dialogue that is kind and understanding. This involves replacing self-critical thoughts or negative self-judgment with more compassionate and self-accepting statements. For example, instead of thinking "I'm such a failure," individuals can consciously shift their thoughts to "Everyone makes mistakes, it's okay to not be perfect." Another strategy is to practice self-care, such as engaging in activities that bring joy or relaxation. This can involve engaging in hobbies, spending time with loved ones, or engaging in self-care rituals such as exercise or meditation. Taking care of one's physical and emotional well-being is an essential component of self-compassion, as it communicates to oneself that one's needs are important and worthy of attention. Cultivating self-compassion is a powerful tool for overcoming insecurity. By treating oneself with kindness, understanding, and acceptance, individuals can learn to challenge and overcome their self-doubt and self-criticism. Self-compassion allows individuals to recognize their own worth and value, regardless of their flaws or failures. It also allows individuals to develop resilience and bounce back from setbacks or failures. Through practicing self-compassion, individuals can begin to develop a more positive and balanced view of themselves, which can ultimately lead to increased confidence and a reduction in feelings of insecurity.

VIII. SEEKING PROFESSIONAL HELP

Many individuals may be hesitant to reach out for assistance, as they may view it as a sign of weakness or failure. Seeking professional help is not only a brave decision but also a necessary one in the journey towards self-improvement. Professionals, such as therapists or counselors, are trained to provide guidance and support in navigating the complexities of insecurity. They possess the necessary expertise to help individuals recognize the underlying causes of their insecurity and develop effective strategies to overcome it. These professionals create a safe and non-judgmental space where individuals can open up about their insecurities and explore the various factors contributing to their feelings of self-doubt. Through therapy or counseling sessions, individuals gain valuable insights into the root causes of their insecurity, whether it be past traumatic experiences or deeply ingrained negative beliefs about themselves. With the guidance of a professional, individuals can challenge these beliefs and replace them with more positive and realistic ones. Addition ally, professionals can help individuals develop coping mechanisms and stress-management techniques to deal with the emotional struggles that often accompany insecurity. This may include Mindfulness exercises, cognitive-behavioral techniques, or other evidence-based approaches that are tailored to the individual's specific needs. Seeking professional help also provides individuals with a dedicated support system. Insecurity can often isolate individuals, making them feel alone in their struggles. By consulting a therapist or counselor, individuals have someone who genuinely listens to their concerns, validates their experiences, and provides the necessary support and encouragement to overcome their insecurities. Professionals can act as a source of accountability, helping individuals stay on track with their progress. They can guide individuals in setting achievable goals and regularly check in to assess their progress, ensuring that they are consistently working towards overcoming their insecurities. Seeking professional help is not a sign of weakness but rather a display of strength and self-awareness. Recognizing that one's insecurities are impacting their overall well-being and taking active steps to address them takes immense courage and determination. By seeking professional help, individuals prioritize their mental health and take control of their lives. They choose to break free from the shackles of insecurity and work towards a future filled with self-confidence and personal growth. Seeking professional help is an essential component in overcoming insecurity. It offers a safe and supportive environment for individuals to explore the underlying causes of their insecurity and develop effective strategies to address it. Professionals provide valuable insights, guidance, and coping mechanisms, helping individuals challenge negative beliefs and develop more positive self-perceptions. Seeking professional help provides individuals with a dedicated support system and ac countability, helping them stay on track in their journey towards self-improvement. Seeking professional help is an act of strength and self-awareness, enabling individuals to regain control of their lives and build a future filled with self-confidence and personal growth.

RECOGNIZING WHEN SELF-HELP METHODS MAY NOT SUFFICE

While self-help methods can be effective in many cases, there are instances where outside support and professional intervention may be necessary. One such situation is when an individual's insecurity stems from deep-rooted psychological issues or traumatic experiences. In these cases, trying to tackle the issue on one's own can be overwhelming and potentially exacerbate the problem. It is essential to recognize when it is time to seek the help of a therapist or counselor who can provide the necessary support and guidance to address these underlying issues.

Another circumstance where self-help methods may not suffice is when an individual's insecurity is perpetuated by negative social influences or toxic relationships. In these situations, no matter how hard one tries to build self-confidence and self-esteem, external factors continue to bring them down. It is important to acknowledge that sometimes, overcoming insecurities requires removing oneself from toxic environments and surrounding oneself with positive, supportive individuals. This could mean cutting ties with toxic friendships or even distancing oneself from toxic family members. Seeking therapy or counseling can be beneficial in learning how to establish healthy boundaries and develop coping strategies for dealing with negative external influences. Self-help methods may not be enough when an individual's insecurity is deeply ingrained in their self-perception and belief system. Negative self-talk and a lack of self-worth may have been ingrained in an individual's psyche from a young age due to various factors such as upbringing, societal pressure, or past traumas. In these cases, it takes more than just reading self-help books or practicing positive affirmations to overcome insecurity. Working with a therapist or counselor who specializes in self-esteem and self-worth can be instrumental in challenging and replacing these negative beliefs with more empowering ones. It often requires a combination of cognitive-behavioral therapy, psychoeducation, and consistent practice to rewire one's perception of oneself and build a healthier sense of self. Self-help methods may fall short when an individual's insecurity is accompanied by mental health disorders such as depression or anxiety. While self-help strategies like exercise, meditation, or journaling can be beneficial in managing these conditions, they may not be sufficient in addressing the root causes of insecurity. Seeking professional help from a therapist or psychiatrist who can provide a comprehensive treatment plan, including therapy, medication, and lifestyle changes, may be necessary to effectively manage these conditions and reduce their impact on one's self-confidence.

Recognizing when self-help methods may not suffice is essential for effectively overcoming insecurity. When insecurities are deeply rooted in psychological issues, perpetuated by negative social influences, ingrained in one's self-perception, or accompanied by mental health disorders, seeking professional support is crucial for lasting change. Self-help methods can be a valuable first step, but knowing when to seek outside help and opening oneself up to professional intervention is a sign of strength and a commitment to personal growth and well-being.

CONSULTING THERAPISTS OR COUNSELORS FOR GUIDANCE

Therapists and counselors are highly trained professionals who possess the knowledge and expertise to help individuals address and work through their insecurities. These professionals use various therapeutic techniques and approaches tailored to the specific needs of their clients. Consulting therapists or counselors can provide individuals with a safe and non-judgmental space to express their insecurities, fears, and concerns. Through this process, individuals can gain a deeper understanding of the root causes of their insecurities and develop strategies to overcome them. Therapists and counselors may utilize cognitive-behavioral therapy (CBT), which focuses on identifying and changing negative thought patterns and behaviors that contribute to insecurity. They may also employ techniques such as exposure therapy, where individuals are gradually exposed to situations that trigger their insecurities in a controlled and supportive environment. This allows individuals to challenge and change their beliefs and fears around certain situations, thus reducing their insecurity. Therapists and counselors can provide valuable guidance and support to individuals in developing healthy coping mechanisms and building self-esteem. By exploring one's own experiences, emotions, and patterns of thought with a therapist or counselor, individuals can gain insight into their insecurities and discover new ways of thinking and behaving that promote emotional well-being and self-assurance. Therapists and counselors often employ a person-centered approach, where the individual's unique needs and experiences are at the forefront of the therapeutic process. This approach allows individuals to feel understood and validated, fostering a sense of trust and rapport with the therapist or counselor. Through this therapeutic relationship, individuals can openly discuss their insecurities and receive guidance that is tailored to their specific circumstances. Therapists and counselors can also provide individuals with practical techniques and tools to manage their insecurities on a day-to-day basis. For instance, they may teach relaxation techniques such as deep breathing exercises or Mindfulness meditation, which can help individuals reduce anxiety and increase their overall sense of well-being. Consulting therapists or counselors for guidance is an effective approach to overcoming insecurity. These professionals possess the expertise and knowledge to help individuals gain a deeper understanding of their insecurities and develop strategies to address and overcome them. By providing a safe and supportive environment, therapists and counselors empower individuals to challenge negative thought patterns and behaviors that contribute to insecurity. Through therapeutic techniques such as cognitive-behavioral therapy and exposure therapy, individuals can gradually reduce their insecurities and develop healthy coping mechanisms. Therapists and counselors offer person-centered support that is tailored to the individual's unique needs and experiences. By working with these professionals, individuals can gain insight into their insecurities, build self-confidence, and develop practical tools to manage insecurities on a daily basis. Seeking guidance from therapists or counselors can be transformative, leading individuals to a more secure and fulfilling life.

UTILIZING RESOURCES AND SUPPORT GROUPS AVAILABLE

One valuable resource is therapy or counseling services, which can provide individuals with a safe space to explore their feelings of insecurity and work towards self-acceptance. Therapists can assist in identifying the root causes of insecurities and develop strategies to address and heal from them. Support groups can be immensely beneficial in providing a sense of community and understanding. These groups often consist of individuals who have experienced similar struggles, creating an environment where participants can share their stories, exchange advice, and offer encouragement. In addition to professional services and support groups, various self-help resources, such as books and podcasts, can offer valuable insights and strategies for building self-confidence. These resources may explore topics such as positive affirmations, Mindfulness, and self-compassion, all of which can aid in challenging and overcoming feelings of insecurity. Educational institutions often provide resources for students dealing with insecurity. College counseling centers typically offer individual therapy sessions, group therapy sessions, and workshops tailored to addressing a wide range of mental health concerns, including insecurity. Academic advisors are available to provide guidance and support, helping students navigate their academic and personal challenges. Universities may also offer mentorship programs where students can connect with older students or faculty members who can serve as mentors and provide guidance and advice. Seeking out these resources and taking advantage of the support available can contribute significantly to an individual's journey towards overcoming insecurity. Utilizing resources and support groups can also help individuals gain a more balanced and realistic perspective regarding their insecurities. Through therapy, counseling, or support groups, individuals can explore and challenge distorted thoughts and negative self-perceptions that fuel insecurity. They can learn cognitive-behavioral techniques to reframe negative thoughts, replacing them with more positive and realistic ones. In support groups, individuals can witness the progress and growth of others who have faced similar challenges, providing hope and inspiration for their own journey. By engaging with resources and support groups, individuals can cultivate a sense of self-compassion and develop skills to counteract insecurities with self-esteem and self-worth.

Overcoming insecurity requires actively seeking out and utilizing the resources and support that are available. Whether it be therapy, support groups, self-help resources, or institutional services, these resources can provide individuals with the tools and guidance necessary for their journey towards self-acceptance and confidence. By engaging in these resources, individuals can gain insight into the root causes of their insecurity, develop strategies for addressing and healing from their insecurities, and challenge negative thought patterns and self-perceptions. Utilizing resources and support groups provides individuals with a sense of community and understanding, enabling them to share their experiences, exchange advice, and offer support to one another. Through these actions, individuals can gradually overcome their insecurities and cultivate a more positive and confident sense of self.

Another strategy to help overcome insecurity is to develop a positive mindset. Insecurities stem from negative thoughts and beliefs about oneself. By replacing these negative thoughts with positive ones, individuals can begin to shift their mindset and conquer their insecurities. One way to cultivate a positive mindset is through affirmations. Affirmations are positive statements that individuals repeat to themselves to help reprogram their subconscious mind. By consistently repeating statements such as "I am worthy," "I am confident," and "I am capable," individuals can begin to internalize these beliefs and boost their self-esteem. Practicing gratitude can also foster a positive mindset. By focusing on the things one is grateful for, individuals can cultivate a sense of appreciation for themselves and their abilities, leading to a more positive self-perception. Adopting a growth mindset can be instrumental in overcoming insecurity. A growth mindset is the belief that abilities and intelligence can be developed through dedication and hard work. Embracing this perspective allows individuals to see setbacks and failures as opportunities for growth rather than indications of their worth. By viewing challenges as learning experiences, individuals can develop resilience and become more secure in their abilities. Surrounding oneself with positive and supportive people can also help combat insecurity. Being around individuals who uplift and encourage can boost self-confidence and provide a sense of validation. These individuals can offer constructive feedback and serve as a source of inspiration, helping individuals recognize their worth and potential. Seeking professional help can be beneficial for those struggling with insecurities. Therapists and counselors are trained to help individuals address their insecurities, explore their underlying causes, and develop strategies for overcoming them. They can provide a safe and nonjudgmental space for individuals to express their concerns, process their feelings, and gain insight into their insecurities. It is important to practice self-care and self-compassion in the journey towards overcoming insecurity. Taking care of one's mental, emotional, and physical well-being is essential for building self-confidence. This can involve engaging in activities that bring joy and relaxation, engaging in regular exercise, getting enough sleep, and practicing self-compassion by being kind and understanding towards oneself. Overcoming insecurity requires a combination of strategies that target one's mindset, relationships, and self-care practices. By actively working towards developing a positive mindset, seeking support from positive individuals and professionals, and practicing self-care, individuals can gradually overcome their insecurities and cultivate a stronger sense of self-worth.

IX. EMBRACING IMPERFECTIONS

In today's society, there seems to be an overwhelming demand for perfection. We are constantly bombarded with images of flawless bodies, perfect homes, and impeccable achievements. It is no wonder that insecurity has become such a prevalent issue in our lives. It is important to remember that perfection is an unattainable goal. Nobody is perfect, and that is perfectly okay. Embracing imperfections is a crucial step in overcoming insecurity. First and foremost, it is important to understand that everyone has flaws. Whether physical or mental, imperfections are what make us human. Society's obsession with perfection has created unrealistic standards that only lead to disappointment and feelings of inadequacy. By embracing our imperfections, we are embracing our authentic selves. Acknowledging our flaws allows us to focus on our strengths and work towards self-improvement in a healthy and sustainable way.

Embracing imperfections also plays a role in building strong relationships. Insecurity often stems from the fear that our shortcomings will be unattractive or unlovable to others. It is our imperfections that often create genuine connections with others. When we allow ourselves to be vulnerable and show our true selves, we invite others to do the same. This fosters an atmosphere of trust and understanding, leading to deeper and more meaningful relationships. By being accepting of our imperfections, we are paving the way for more authentic connections with others. Embracing imperfections also leads to a greater sense of self-acceptance and self-love. Insecurity often stems from a lack of confidence in ourselves. We may constantly compare ourselves to others or feel like we never measure up to societal standards. By acknowledging our imperfections, we are accepting ourselves as we are. This self-acceptance allows us to let go of the need for external validation and find contentment within ourselves. When we learn to love ourselves, flaws and all, we become more resilient and better equipped to face life's challenges. Embracing imperfections opens the door to growth and personal development. When we are constantly striving for perfection, we often become paralyzed by the fear of failure. We may avoid trying new things or taking risks because we are afraid of making mistakes. It is through our imperfections and failures that we learn the most valuable lessons. By embracing imperfections, we become more resilient, adaptable, and open to new experiences. We learn to appreciate the journey rather than solely focusing on the end result. This mindset not only allows for personal growth but also fosters creativity and innovation. Embracing imperfections is a powerful tool in overcoming insecurity. By letting go of the unrealistic expectation of perfection, we can learn to accept ourselves as we are. This acceptance not only leads to stronger relationships but also fosters self-acceptance and personal growth. It is in our imperfections that we find our true strength and beauty. So let us celebrate our flaws and embrace the imperfect journey of life.

ACCEPTING ONESELF AS A WORK IN PROGRESS

While it may be difficult to accept oneself as a work in progress, it is an essential step towards overcoming insecurity. Individuals struggling with insecurity hold themselves to unrealistic standards of perfection. They believe that any flaws or imperfections in their character or appearance make them unworthy or less valuable. It is important to recognize that no one is perfect, and as humans, we are naturally inclined to make mistakes and learn from them. Accepting oneself as a work in progress means embracing the journey of self-improvement and understanding that growth is a lifelong process. This mindset allows for a more compassionate and forgiving attitude towards oneself, as it acknowledges that hiccups and setbacks are a normal part of personal development. Accepting oneself as a work in progress fosters a mentality of continuous learning and self-reflection. Instead of critiquing oneself harshly, individuals begin to view their shortcomings as opportunities for growth and change. By recognizing areas that require improvement, one can set goals and work towards becoming the best version of themselves. This process of self-development promotes personal growth, leading to increased self-esteem and a sense of fulfillment. Accepting oneself as a work in progress enables individuals to focus on their strengths and accomplishments rather than fixating on their shortcomings. By acknowledging that one is not defined solely by their flaws, individuals can appreciate and celebrate their unique qualities and talents. This shift in perspective can immensely boost self-confidence and diminish feelings of insecurity. Accepting oneself as a work in progress allows individuals to cultivate a healthier relationship with themselves and with others. When individuals recognize that they are not expected to be perfect, they can let go of the constant need for validation and approval from others. Instead, they can engage in more authentic and meaningful connections, as their self-worth is no longer dependent on others' opinions. Accepting oneself as a work in progress creates a mindset of acceptance and empathy towards others. By understanding that everyone is on their own journey of self-improvement, individuals become more understanding and compassionate towards others' flaws and shortcomings. This cultivates a community of support and encouragement, where individuals can uplift and empower each other to reach their fullest potential. Accepting oneself as a work in progress is an essential step towards overcoming insecurity. It allows for self-compassion, continuous learning, and growth. By recognizing and embracing one's flaws and imperfections as opportunities for development, individuals can focus on their strengths and accomplishments, leading to increased self-esteem and fulfillment. Accepting oneself as a work in progress fosters healthier relationships and a more empathetic and supportive community. By embracing the journey of self-improvement, individuals can navigate through life with confidence, resilience, and a sense of self-worth.

CELEBRATING ACHIEVEMENTS, NO MATTER HOW SMALL

Achievements plays a significant role in overcoming insecurities. It is natural to feel discouraged by self-doubt and the fear of failure, but acknowledging and celebrating even the smallest accomplishments can greatly boost self-confidence and motivate individuals to continue striving for success. When individuals acknowledge their achievements, it acts as validation for their efforts and capabilities, providing them with a sense of accomplishment. Celebrating achievements, regardless of their scale, not only fosters a positive mindset, but it also establishes a sense of self-worth and reaffirms one's capabilities. For instance, an individual who lacks confidence in their writing abilities might find it intimidating to share their work with others. If they receive positive feedback or recognition for their writing from a friend or a teacher, it can validate their skills and encourage them to pursue their passion further. This validation helps in silencing the inner voice of insecurity and fuels the belief that one can achieve their goals. Celebrating achievements, no matter how small, enables individuals to recognize their progress and growth. People tend to focus on the long-term goals, which can be overwhelming and discouraging. By disregarding smaller milestones, individuals fail to acknowledge the smaller steps that lead them towards achieving their ultimate objective. By celebrating even the smallest of achievements, individuals become more self-aware and gain a better perspective into their journey. For example, a student who struggles with public speaking might set a goal of delivering a flawless presentation. Though perfection might not be achieved immediately, the student can celebrate conquering small hurdles, such as speaking confidently for a minute or receiving positive feedback on their body language. By recognizing these milestones, the student's self-confidence increases, allowing them to gradually overcome their fear and become an effective public speaker. Celebrating achievements, no matter how small, encourages individuals to set realistic goals and aids in overcoming the fear of failure. Insecurities stem from setting unrealistic expectations and experiencing disappointments when these expectations are not met. By celebrating small wins and acknowledging incremental progress, individuals can develop a healthier and more realistic approach to achieving their goals. This approach fosters a growth mindset that embraces failures as learning opportunities, rather than reflections of personal shortcomings. For instance, an athlete may set a goal of running a marathon but may struggle with maintaining the desired pace. By recognizing the smaller milestones, such as shaving off seconds in their lap timings or completing a longer distance, the athlete becomes more motivated to improve and can eventually accomplish their ultimate goal. Thus, celebrating small achievements enhances one's sense of self-worth, encourages personal growth, and enables the development of a realistic and positive mindset that fosters resilience and perseverance. Celebrating achievements, regardless of their magnitude, is crucial in overcoming insecurities. It acts as validation of one's efforts and capabilities, promotes growth and progress, and fosters a positive and realistic mindset that helps individuals overcome their fear of failure. By recognizing and celebrating small achievements, individuals can cultivate a sense of self-worth and build confidence, effectively overcoming their insecurities and paving the way for future success.

EMBRACING FLAWS AS PART OF ONE'S UNIQUENESS

Society often perpetuates an idealized image of perfection, leading individuals to believe that their flaws are undesirable or unworthy. It is essential to recognize that flaws are what make each person unique and authentic. Embracing imperfections allows individuals to develop self-acceptance, fostering a positive self-image and leading to increased confidence. Flaws provide opportunities for growth and self-improvement. When individuals identify their flaws, they become aware of areas where they can strive for personal development and, ultimately, become better versions of themselves. By acknowledging and embracing flaws, one can become more understanding and empathetic towards others, fostering a sense of inclusivity and breaking down societal standards for perfection. Rather than striving for unattainable perfection, individuals should focus on embracing their flaws as integral parts of their identities. Embracing flaws requires a shift in paradigm, as it challenges societal norms and expectations. Society often equates flaws with weakness, while in reality, they are a testament to one's resilience and strength. Recognizing flaws as unique traits and characteristics allows individuals to challenge society's shallow notions of beauty and perfection. Truly embracing flaws involves not only accepting them but celebrating them as integral features of one's identity. This celebration of flaws aids in building a strong sense of self-worth, as individuals realize that they are more than their imperfections.

Embracing flaws enables individuals to cultivate authenticity and genuine connections with others. In a world where images are heavily edited and filtered, embracing flaws is a radical act of self-love and authenticity. Vulnerability and open self-acceptance create an environment that encourages others to do the same, fostering deeper connections and relationships. By showing others that flaws are not to be hidden but celebrated, individuals contribute to a more inclusive society that values diversity in all its forms. Embracing flaws also plays a critical role in personal growth and self-improvement. When individuals acknowledge their flaws, they can identify areas where they can work on themselves. Rather than becoming stagnant or complacent, embracing flaws fuels a desire to grow and learn. Accepting that flaws are not indicative of failure, but rather opportunities for growth, allows individuals to adopt a growth mindset. This mindset promotes continuous improvement, encouraging individuals to recognize their flaws and actively work towards self-improvement. Embracing flaws as part of one's uniqueness is crucial for overcoming insecurity. Society's standards of perfection can be damaging to individuals' self-esteem, causing them to view their flaws as undesirable. Embracing flaws allows individuals to develop self-acceptance, fosters a positive self-image, and increases confidence. Embracing flaws creates an environment of inclusivity, authenticity, and personal growth. When individuals acknowledge and celebrate their flaws, they break free from societal expectations and embrace their authentic selves. By embracing flaws, individuals contribute to a more inclusive society that values diversity and recognizes the beauty in imperfection.

One of the most effective ways to overcome insecurity is by cultivating self-compassion. Self-compassion involves treating oneself with the same kindness and understanding that one would offer to a close friend or loved one. Individuals who struggle with insecurity are overly self-critical, constantly berating themselves for perceived inadequacies or failures. By practicing self-compassion, individuals can learn to recognize and challenge these negative self-judgments, ultimately fostering a more positive and accepting self-image. Research has shown that self-compassion is strongly associated with greater psychological well-being and resilience. In a study conducted by Neff and Vonk (2009), participants who scored higher on measures of self-compassion reported lower levels of trait anxiety and depression. Individuals high in self-compassion demonstrated greater emotional intelligence, empathy, and social connectedness. These findings suggest that self-compassion not only helps combat insecurity but also cultivates important emotional and interpersonal skills. One way to develop self-compassion is through self-care practices. Engaging in activities that promote physical, emotional, and mental well-being can help individuals cultivate self-compassion by demonstrating a commitment to self-care and self-worth. Examples of self-care practices include exercise, Mindfulness meditation, journaling, and engaging in hobbies or activities that bring joy and fulfillment. These practices not only allow individuals to take time for themselves but also offer an opportunity to nurture a positive relationship with oneself. By prioritizing self-care, individuals can begin to challenge the belief that they are unworthy or undeserving of love and compassion. Individuals can enhance their self-compassion by reframing negative self-talk and replacing it with self-encouragement and acceptance. Insecurity stems from internalized negative beliefs and self-doubt. By consciously acknowledging and challenging these beliefs, individuals can begin to replace them with more positive and affirming thoughts. For example, instead of berating oneself for making a mistake, one can choose to recognize that everyone makes errors and view it as an opportunity to learn and grow. By reframing negative self-talk, individuals can foster self-compassion and build a more resilient and constructive mindset. In addition to self-care practices and reframing, building strong social support networks can also be instrumental in overcoming insecurity. Surrounding oneself with supportive and uplifting individuals can offer validation, encouragement, and a sense of belonging. Friends and loved ones can act as a buffer against self-doubt and provide guidance and perspective when facing challenges or setbacks. Participating in support groups or seeking therapy can offer additional resources and strategies to address insecurity. By connecting with others who have similar experiences, individuals can gain insights and strategies for managing insecurity, ultimately fostering a stronger sense of self-worth and security. Overcoming insecurity requires a multifaceted approach that combines self-compassion, self-care practices, reframing negative self-talk, and building social support networks. By cultivating self-compassion, individuals can challenge negative self-judgments, fostering a more positive and accepting self-image. Engaging in self-care practices demonstrates a commitment to self-worth and well-being, while reframing negative self-talk allows for the development of a more constructive mindset. Building strong social support networks provides validation, encouragement, and a sense of belonging. By implementing these strategies, individuals can overcome inse-

curity and cultivate a greater sense of self-confidence and resilience.

X. PRACTICING SELF-CARE

Self-care is an essential component of overcoming insecurity and promoting overall wellbeing. Engaging in self-care activities helps individuals maintain a healthy balance between physical, emotional, and mental health. By dedicating time and effort to prioritize self-care, individuals can cultivate a stronger sense of self-worth and confidence, thus combating insecurity. One crucial aspect of self-care is taking care of one's physical health. Regular exercise, adequate sleep, and a balanced diet contribute to physical well-being, which in turn positively impacts mental and emotional health. Engaging in physical activity not only improves physical fitness but also releases endorphins, commonly known as the "feel-good" hormones, which reduce stress and enhance mood. Ensuring that one gets sufficient rest and follows a nutritious diet can greatly impact energy levels and overall outlook on life.

In addition to addressing physical health, self-care also encompasses paying attention to one's emotional needs. Emotions play a significant role in shaping an individual's perception of oneself and the world. Consequently, it is important to recognize and express emotions in a healthy and constructive way. Engaging in activities that promote emotional well-being, such as journaling, practicing Mindfulness, or seeking therapy, can aid in developing emotional intelligence and resilience. Journaling provides an outlet for introspection and self-reflection, allowing individuals to explore their thoughts and feelings, and gain insights into their insecurities. Likewise, practicing Mindfulness cultivates self-awareness and teaches individuals to accept their vulnerability without judgment. Therapy, whether individual or group, offers a supportive and non-judgmental environment wherein individuals can explore the root causes of their insecurities and work towards overcoming them.

Self-care involves nurturing one's mental health. Insecurities often stem from negative self-talk and irrational beliefs. Engaging in activities that promote positive thinking, such as reading inspirational books or listening to motivational podcasts, can help challenge and reframe negative thoughts, fostering a more positive mindset. Engaging in hobbies and activities that provide intellectual stimulation not only enhances cognitive skills but also brings joy and a sense of accomplishment. Taking time for oneself and engaging in activities that bring pleasure and satisfaction contribute to overall mental well-being, which has a direct impact on one's self-confidence and ability to overcome insecurity. Practicing self-care requires self-compassion and a commitment to prioritizing one's own well-being. It involves letting go of external pressures and expectations and focusing on what truly nourishes the mind, body, and soul. By dedicating time and effort to self-care, individuals can create a foundation of self-love and acceptance, which serves as a powerful tool in overcoming insecurity. Self-care is not a selfish act but rather a necessary one in order to thrive in all aspects of life. It is through the practice of self-care that individuals can navigate the complexities of life with a greater sense of security and self-assuredness. In doing so, they will not only enjoy a more fulfilling and balanced life themselves but also be better equipped to support and uplift others.

TAKING CARE OF PHYSICAL HEALTH THROUGH EXERCISE AND PROPER NUTRITION

Regular exercise not only improves physical fitness but also has a profound impact on mental well-being. Engaging in physical activity releases endorphins, commonly known as the "feel-good" hormones, which can alleviate symptoms of depression and anxiety. Exercise promotes better sleep patterns, which are essential for maintaining a stable mood and managing stress levels. By incorporating exercise into daily routines, individuals can develop a sense of accomplishment and improve self-confidence, ultimately helping them to overcome insecurities.

Proper nutrition is equally important in fostering physical and mental well-being. Consuming a balanced diet ensures that the body receives the necessary nutrients to function optimally. Nutrient-rich foods, such as fruits, vegetables, whole grains, lean proteins, and healthy fats, provide the body with essential vitamins and minerals. These nutrients are vital for maintaining energy levels, supporting brain function, and promoting overall physical health. A well-balanced diet can positively impact one's self-image and body confidence, thus reducing feelings of insecurity. In addition to the immediate benefits, exercise and proper nutrition contribute to long-term physical health. Regular physical activity lowers the risk of chronic diseases, such as cardiovascular diseases, obesity, and diabetes. It improves cardiovascular and respiratory function, enhances bone density, and strengthens muscles and joints. Likewise, a healthy diet can prevent the onset of various health conditions, such as high blood pressure, high cholesterol, and certain types of cancer. By prioritizing exercise and proper nutrition, individuals can enhance their overall well-being and reduce the likelihood of developing physical health issues, providing them with a sense of control and security in their bodies. Engaging in exercise and maintaining a healthy diet can have a profound impact on one's self-esteem. As individuals see improvements in their physical appearance, endurance, and overall fitness level, their confidence and self-worth are likely to increase. Taking ownership of one's health and well-being by choosing to exercise and eat nutritiously can provide a sense of empowerment, ultimately aiding in the journey of overcoming insecurities. Taking care of physical health through exercise and proper nutrition is a crucial step towards overcoming insecurity. Regular exercise releases endorphins, improves sleep patterns, and promotes a sense of accomplishment, all of which can positively impact mental well-being. Proper nutrition, on the other hand, supports physical health, provides essential nutrients, and contributes to a positive self-image. By incorporating exercise and a balanced diet into daily routines, individuals can enhance their physical fitness, reduce the risk of chronic diseases, and boost their self-esteem, ultimately aiding in the journey of overcoming insecurities and cultivating a healthier sense of self.

ENGAGING IN ACTIVITIES THAT BRING JOY AND RELAXATION

In today's fast-paced, competitive world, it is easy to become overwhelmed and succumb to self-doubt. By finding activities that bring joy and relaxation, individuals can counteract these negative emotions and build a sense of self-confidence. One such activity is practicing Mindfulness and meditation. Mindfulness allows individuals to focus on the present moment, cultivating a greater awareness of their thoughts and emotions. Through regular practice, individuals can learn to observe their insecurities without judgment, allowing them to let go of these negative thoughts and embrace a more positive mindset. Engaging in physical exercise is another effective way to alleviate insecurity. Exercise releases endorphins, or "feel-good" hormones, which can improve mood and boost self-esteem. Whether it is going for a jog, taking a yoga class, or hitting the gym, incorporating regular exercise into one's routine can promote a sense of accomplishment and overall well-being. Finding activities that bring joy can significantly impact one's sense of self-worth. For example, engaging in a hobby or pursuing a passion can instill a sense of purpose and fulfillment. Whether it be painting, playing an instrument, or writing poetry, allowing oneself to immerse in these activities can provide a much-needed escape from insecurities and allow for self-expression. Spending time with loved ones and engaging in social activities is essential in combating insecurity. Sharing moments with friends and family who genuinely care can help restore one's confidence and remind them of their inherent worth. Engaging in activities such as going for a meal, watching a movie, or simply having a meaningful conversation can foster a sense of belonging and support. Surrounding oneself with positive influences and role models can also play a crucial role in overcoming insecurity. By seeking out individuals who radiate confidence and exhibit healthy self-esteem, one can learn valuable lessons and adopt similar traits. Such individuals can serve as mentors, providing guidance and encouragement throughout the process. When faced with insecurity, it is important to remember that overcoming it is a gradual and ongoing journey. Engaging in activities that bring joy and relaxation is a vital step that can empower individuals to overcome their insecurities and lead a more fulfilling life. By practicing Mindfulness, engaging in physical exercise, pursuing hobbies and passions, spending time with loved ones, and seeking positive influences, individuals can cultivate a stronger sense of self-confidence and learn to embrace their inner worth. The process of overcoming insecurity involves self-acceptance and acknowledging that everyone has flaws and insecurities. By focusing on personal growth and surrounding oneself with positive influences, individuals can gradually overcome their insecurities and reach their full potential.

PRIORITIZING SLEEP AND MANAGING STRESS LEVELS

Sleep plays an essential role in maintaining emotional and mental well-being. When we are sleep-deprived, our emotional resilience is compromised, and insecurities can intensify. Adequate sleep ensures that our brain functions optimally, improving our ability to cope with stress and setbacks. Managing stress levels is essential because stress can be a significant trigger for feelings of insecurity. Chronic stress activates the body's fight-or-flight response, leading to the release of stress hormones such as cortisol. Elevated levels of cortisol can impact our self-esteem and self-confidence, exacerbating feelings of insecurity. Developing healthy sleep habits and stress management techniques can greatly contribute to overcoming insecurity. To prioritize sleep, it is vital to establish a consistent sleep schedule. Going to bed and waking up at the same time each day helps regulate our body's internal clock, improving the quality of our sleep. Creating a relaxing pre-sleep routine, such as reading a book or taking a warm bath, can also signal our body that it is time to wind down. It is important to avoid stimulating activities, such as looking at screens or engaging in intense exercise, close to bedtime, as these can interfere with our ability to fall asleep. Maintaining an optimal sleep environment, with a comfortable mattress, pillows, and a dark and quiet room, can facilitate a restful night's sleep, allowing us to wake up feeling refreshed and better equipped to tackle insecurities. Alongside prioritizing sleep, managing stress levels is crucial in overcoming insecurity. One effective stress management technique is adopting a regular exercise routine. Engaging in physical activity releases endorphins, our body's natural mood boosters, reducing stress and anxiety. Exercise also promotes better sleep, which, as discussed earlier, is vital in addressing feelings of insecurity. Practicing relaxation techniques, such as deep breathing exercises, Mindfulness meditation, and yoga, can help calm the mind and reduce stress. These techniques allow us to develop a greater sense of self-awareness, understanding, and acceptance, diminishing the power of insecurities in our lives. In addition to these individual strategies, seeking professional support, such as therapy or counseling, can greatly assist in managing stress and overcoming insecurity. Therapists can provide guidance and tools for building self-esteem, challenging negative thoughts, and developing coping mechanisms to deal with stressors. Working with a therapist can also help uncover the root causes of insecurity, enabling individuals to address and heal underlying issues. Prioritizing sleep and managing stress levels are pivotal in overcoming insecurity. Adequate sleep promotes emotional resilience and helps regulate our emotions, while managing stress prevents its detrimental effects on self-esteem and confidence. Developing healthy sleep habits and utilizing stress management techniques, such as exercise and relaxation practices, can significantly contribute to conquering feelings of insecurity. Seeking professional support through therapy can also provide invaluable guidance and assistance in addressing and healing underlying issues. By prioritizing our well-being and implementing effective strategies, we can foster a positive self-image, build resilience, and overcome insecurity.

One of the key components to overcoming insecurity is developing a strong confident mindset. Insecurity often stems from a lack of confidence in one's abilities or self-worth, and by actively working to build confidence, individuals can begin to combat their insecurities. Building confidence starts by acknowledging and accepting one's strengths and accomplishments. This can be done by reflecting on past achievements, no matter how small, and recognizing the skills and qualities that contributed to those successes. In addition, seeking validation from others can often perpetuate feelings of insecurity. Instead, individuals should focus on cultivating self-validation by setting personal goals and celebrating their own achievements. Another effective strategy for building confidence is by stepping out of one's comfort zone. By facing challenges and taking risks, individuals can prove to themselves that they are capable of handling difficult situations. This can be as simple as trying a new hobby or taking on a leadership role in a project. Engaging in activities that promote self-care and self-improvement can enhance confidence. This can include exercise, practicing Mindfulness, or pursuing further education or certifications. By investing time and effort into personal growth, individuals can boost their self-image and develop greater self-assurance. It is crucial to surround oneself with a supportive network of friends, family, or mentors. Having people who believe in one's abilities and provide positive reinforcement can help to counteract feelings of insecurity. These support systems can offer guidance, encouragement, and constructive feedback, which can be instrumental in building confidence. It is equally important to distance oneself from toxic individuals or situations that may contribute to feelings of insecurity. Insecurities can often be heightened by comparisons to others. The constant need to measure up to others' achievements or appearances can be detrimental to one's self-esteem. Instead of comparing oneself to others, individuals should focus on their own journey and progress. Recognizing that everyone has their own unique strengths and weaknesses can help to shift the focus away from comparison and towards personal growth. Embracing vulnerability can be a powerful tool in overcoming insecurity. Opening up about one's fears and insecurities to trusted individuals can foster deeper connections and provide support in times of need. It is important to remember that vulnerability is not a sign of weakness but rather an avenue for growth and self-acceptance. Practicing self-compassion is essential in overcoming insecurity. It is natural to experience setbacks or failures, but instead of berating oneself, individuals should practice self-kindness and respond to these moments with understanding and self-encouragement. By treating oneself with the same compassion and understanding as one would extend to a close friend, individuals can foster a sense of self-acceptance and resilience. Overcoming insecurity is a journey that requires self-reflection, personal development, and the cultivation of a confident mindset. By actively implementing these strategies, individuals can begin to break free from the shackles of insecurity and lead a more fulfilling and confident life.

XI. STEPPING OUT OF COMFORT ZONES

In order to overcome insecurity, one must be willing to step out of their comfort zones. Comfort zones are considered safe havens where individuals feel secure and in control, but they can also become barriers that hinder personal growth and development. Stepping out of comfort zones allows individuals to experience new challenges, learn from failures, and build resilience. It requires a willingness to take risks and face uncertainty, knowing that growth and self-improvement are waiting on the other side. Stepping out of comfort zones often involves engaging in activities or situations that may initially induce fear or anxiety. Whether it is giving a presentation in front of a large audience, participating in a group discussion, or pursuing a new hobby or interest, stepping out of one's comfort zone is essential. The first step in stepping out of comfort zones is to identify the areas in which one feels limited or boxed in by their insecurities. Personal reflection and self-awareness are crucial for this step, as they allow individuals to recognize the specific fears or anxieties that hold them back. By acknowledging these limitations, individuals can then begin to work on expanding their comfort zones and tackling their insecurities head-on.

Once the areas of insecurity are identified, it is important to take small steps towards stepping out of the comfort zone. Setting achievable goals and gradually increasing the level of difficulty in each new challenge can significantly contribute to one's confidence and willingness to step further. For instance, a person who is afraid of public speaking can start by giving a presentation to a smaller group of trusted friends or colleagues, and gradually work their way up to larger audiences. By breaking down the challenge into smaller, manageable steps, individuals can build a solid foundation of confidence in their abilities.

Another effective strategy for stepping out of comfort zones is seeking support and encouragement from others. Sharing one's fears and insecurities with trusted friends, family, or mentors can provide a much-needed boost of motivation and reassurance. Surrounding oneself with a positive and supportive network can also provide a safety net in case of failures or setbacks, helping individuals to bounce back and persist in their efforts to step out of their comfort zones.

It is important to note that stepping out of comfort zones is a process, and not something that can be achieved overnight. It requires perseverance, patience, and a commitment to personal growth. Each step forward, no matter how small, should be celebrated as a victory. Over time, with consistent practice and a willingness to embrace discomfort, individuals can gradually expand their comfort zones and overcome their insecurities.

Stepping out of comfort zones is an essential step towards overcoming insecurity. It requires individuals to identify their limitations, set achievable goals, seek support, and embrace discomfort. Though it may be challenging and anxiety-inducing at first, stepping out of comfort zones leads to person al growth, enhanced self-confidence, and increased resilience. By continually pushing the boundaries of comfort, individuals can break free from the debilitating grasp of insecurity and unlock their full potential.

CHALLENGING ONESELF TO FACE FEARS AND TAKE RISKS

By deliberately putting ourselves in uncomfortable situations, we can push the boundaries of our comfort zones and grow in the process. When we challenge ourselves to face our fears, whether it be public speaking, trying something new, or confronting a difficult situation, we prove to ourselves that we are capable of handling adversity. This process requires us to acknowledge our insecurities and confront them head-on with courage and determination. Taking risks also allows us to expand our horizons and open ourselves up to new experiences and opportunities. It is through these challenges and risks that we learn valuable life lessons and develop a sense of resilience and self-confidence. It is important to note that the process of facing fears and taking risks may not always result in immediate success. It is natural to encounter obstacles and setbacks along the way. Nevertheless, it is through these failures that we gain valuable insight and learn how to adapt and grow. By persisting and persevering through these challenges, we can develop a mindset focused on growth and self-improvement. Challenging oneself to face fears and take risks also allows us to gain a sense of empowerment and control over our lives. When we confront our insecurities, we no longer allow them to control us. Instead, we take ownership of our fears and actively work towards overcoming them. This process not only strengthens our sense of self, but it also boosts our self-esteem and self-worth. By facing our fears head-on, we demonstrate to ourselves and others that we are strong-willed and capable individuals. In addition, challenging ourselves also helps to build resilience. It is through the experience of taking risks and facing fear that we learn how to bounce back from setbacks and adapt to new challenges. We become better equipped to handle adversity and setbacks, and we develop the ability to persevere in the face of difficulty. Challenging oneself to face fears and take risks is crucial in overcoming insecurity. By pushing the limits of our comfort zones, we can grow, learn, and develop the necessary skills to overcome our insecurities. It is important to remember that this process will not be easy, and setbacks and failures are inevitable. It is through these challenges that we gain valuable insight and build resilience. By confronting our fears head-on, we take control of our lives and develop a strong sense of self. In time, we will emerge stronger, more confident, and better equipped to face any future insecurities that may arise. The journey to overcoming insecurity starts with taking that first step, and it is through challenging oneself that true growth and self-empowerment can be achieved.

TRYING NEW EXPERIENCES TO EXPAND PERSONAL BOUNDARIES

Stepping out of one's comfort zone allows individuals to challenge their preconceived limitations and discover untapped potential. By actively seeking out new experiences, individuals have the opportunity to face their fears in a controlled and supportive environment. For instance, someone who is insecure about public speaking can join a public speaking club or take a class that focuses on building confidence in this area. Through persistent practice and exposure to public speaking situations, they can gradually overcome their insecurity and become more confident speakers. Trying new experiences broadens horizons and exposes individuals to different perspectives and ideas, enabling them to grow as individuals. When they push themselves to venture into unfamiliar territory, they become more adaptable and open-minded, leading them to develop a sense of self-assurance and resilience. Seeking new experiences encourages personal growth and fosters a sense of accomplishment. Whether it be learning a new language, traveling to a foreign country, or taking up a new hobby, these endeavours allow individuals to step outside their comfort zone and build their self-esteem through tangible achievements. The sense of mastery gained from conquering new challenges can boost confidence levels and gradually chip away at insecurities. Trying new experiences nurtures creativity and fosters personal development. When individuals actively seek out novel experiences, they cultivate a sense of curiosity and explore different aspects of their identity. They may discover hidden talents or passions that they were previously unaware of, thus boosting their self-confidence. For example, someone who has always been re-served may decide to join a drama class and discover a passion for acting. Through this experience, they not only overcome their fear of being in the spotlight but also gain a newfound sense of self-assurance through their talent as an actor. Trying new ex-periences to expand personal boundaries is a valuable strategy for overcoming insecurity. By embracing unfamiliar situations, individuals can challenge their preconceived limitations and discover hidden potential. Stepping outside the comfort zone allows for the exposure to new ideas and perspectives, fostering personal growth and expanding one's horizons. Venturing into uncharted territory provides opportunities for personal achievements, which can boost self-confidence and chip away at insecurities. Actively seeking new experiences also promotes creativity and self-discovery, allowing individuals to explore different aspects of their identity and develop a stronger sense of self-assurance. Embracing novel experiences is an effective way to overcome insecurity and build a confident, resilient self.

CELEBRATING PERSONAL GROWTH ACHIEVED BY STEPPING OUTSIDE COMFORT ZONES

Oftentimes, individuals find themselves living within the boundaries of their comfort zones as a result of fear and self-doubt. This limited existence can hinder personal growth and prevent individuals from reaching their full potential. By taking the courageous step to venture beyond their comfort zones, individuals open themselves up to new experiences and opportunities for personal development. This process of pushing beyond boundaries can be intimidating and uncomfortable, as it requires individuals to face their fears and confront their insecurities head-on. Overcoming these obstacles allows individuals to develop resilience, build self-confidence, and broaden their perspectives. When individuals step outside their comfort zones, they are forced to confront their fears and insecurities. This process is not easy, as it requires individuals to push past their self-imposed limitations and confront the unknown. By facing these fears, individuals can gain a greater sense of self-assurance and belief in their abilities. Each new experience outside the comfort zone serves as a reminder of the strength and resilience that lie within. Regardless of the outcome, celebrating the mere act of stepping outside the comfort zone is an important step in overcoming insecurity. In addition to building confidence, stepping outside the comfort zone allows individuals to expand their horizons and broaden their perspectives. By engaging in activities or pursuing opportunities that are unfamiliar or challenging, individuals expose themselves to new ideas and ways of thinking. This exposure can lead to personal growth and allow individuals to develop a greater appreciation for diversity and the richness of human experience. By celebrating personal growth achieved through stepping outside the comfort zone, individuals foster a mindset of continuous learning and growth.

Personal growth achieved through stepping outside the comfort zone not only benefits individuals, but also those around them. As individuals become more confident and open to new experiences, they often inspire and encourage others to do the same. By celebrating their personal achievements, individuals serve as role models for those struggling with their own insecurities. This celebration of growth, in turn, can create a positive ripple effect within communities, as individuals are more likely to support and uplift one another in their pursuit of personal development.

Celebrating personal growth achieved by stepping outside comfort zones is a crucial element in overcoming insecurity. By pushing beyond the boundaries of what is familiar and comfortable, individuals can cultivate resilience, confidence, and a broader perspective. Although venturing outside the comfort zone can be challenging, it is through these experiences that individuals can truly grow and develop. By embracing and celebrating these achievements, individuals can inspire others and create a culture of continuous growth and support. It is imperative that individuals recognize and celebrate the power of stepping outside the comfort zone in their journey towards overcoming insecurity and achieving personal growth.

Another effective strategy to overcome insecurity is to practice self-compassion. Self-compassion involves treating oneself with kindness, understanding, and patience, rather than being self-critical and judgmental. Research has shown that individuals who are more self-compassionate have higher levels of self-esteem and overall well-being. To cultivate self-compassion, one can start by recognizing and acknowledging their own feelings of insecurity without judgment or self-blame. It is important to remember that insecurities are a natural part of being human and everyone experiences them to some extent. Taking a compassionate approach towards oneself can help to alleviate the negative emotions associated with insecurity and foster a sense of self-acceptance and self-worth. Another aspect of practicing self-compassion involves reframing negative self-talk and replacing it with more positive and affirming thoughts. Instead of allowing the inner critic to dictate one's self-perception, it is essential to challenge these negative thoughts and replace them with statements of self-love and encouragement. This process may take time and effort, but through consistent practice, individuals can gradually rewire their mindset and develop a more compassionate and empowering inner dialogue. Building healthy and supportive relationships is crucial in overcoming insecurity. Surrounding oneself with a strong support network can provide reassurance and validation, which can help to counteract feelings of self-doubt and insecurity. It is important to seek out individuals who genuinely care about one's well-being and who can offer constructive feedback and encouragement. Developing these types of relationships can contribute to a sense of belonging and acceptance, ultimately boosting one's self-confidence and mitigating insecurities. Engaging in open and honest communication with trusted friends, family members, or a therapist can provide an opportunity to share insecurities and fears, allowing for vulnerability and emotional support. By sharing personal experiences with others, individuals can often find that they are not alone in their struggles and that their feelings of insecurity are not unique or abnormal. Insecurity can significantly impact an individual's well-being and overall quality of life. By implementing various strategies, insecurity can be effectively addressed and ultimately overcome. Embracing self-awareness and self-acceptance, challenging negative self-talk, and practicing self-compassion are key components in navigating and overcoming insecurities. Building strong and supportive relationships can provide validation and reassurance, bolstering one's sense of self-worth and confidence. While overcoming insecurity may require time, effort, and consistent practice, the rewards are well worth the investment. By taking proactive steps to combat insecurity, individuals can experience personal growth, increased self-confidence, and a more fulfilling life.

XII. FOSTERING A SUPPORTIVE INNER DIALOGUE

Our thoughts and beliefs about ourselves greatly influence how we perceive ourselves and our abilities. It is crucial to cultivate a positive and nurturing inner voice. This can be done by regularly challenging negative self-talk and replacing it with more constructive and compassionate thoughts. For instance, instead of dwelling on past failures and mistakes, individuals can remind themselves of their past successes and achievements. By focusing on their strengths and accomplishments, they can boost their self-confidence and combat feelings of insecurity. It is essential to adopt a growth mindset—an attitude that embraces challenges and considers setbacks as learning opportunities. This mindset allows individuals to see their worth beyond external validation and to realize that they are capable of growth and improvement. Cultivating a supportive inner dialogue also involves practicing self-compassion. Instead of berating themselves when they make a mistake or experience a setback, individuals should offer themselves understanding and kindness. Treating oneself with compassion creates a sense of safety and acceptance, enabling individuals to embrace their vulnerability and manage their insecurities in healthier ways.

In fostering a supportive inner dialogue, cognitive behavioral therapy holds a valuable framework for individuals to challenge and reframe their negative thoughts. The first step is to identify and become aware of negative self-defeating thoughts as they arise. This requires Mindfulness and self-reflection, as individuals need to pay attention to their inner chatter. Once negative thoughts are identified, individuals can question their validity and challenge them with evidence that contradicts them. For example, if someone believes they are not good enough to succeed in a specific field, they can challenge this thought by remembering times when they demonstrated competence and achieved success in other areas. Individuals can probe deeper to understand the underlying beliefs that fuel negative thoughts, such as a fear of judgment or rejection. By deconstructing these beliefs, individuals can start to gradually replace them with more positive and empowering ones. It is essential to practice affirmations and positive self-talk regularly. By intentionally repeating uplifting and motivating statements, individuals can rewire their thought patterns over time and cultivate a more supportive inner dialogue. To effectively foster a supportive inner dialogue, it is also critical to seek and maintain a supportive network of people who uplift and inspire. Surrounding oneself with individuals who believe in one's potential and provide encouragement and validation is incredibly empowering. These individuals can offer a different perspective, challenge negative self-perceptions, and provide a source of emotional support. Building such connections can be achieved by actively seeking out like-minded individuals, participating in supportive communities or groups, and being open and vulnerable about one's struggles and aspirations. Seeking support from professionals such as therapists or counselors can provide valuable guidance and tools for fostering a supportive inner dialogue.

Fostering a supportive inner dialogue is integral to overcoming insecurity. By challenging negative self-talk, cultivating a growth mindset, practicing self-compassion, and seeking support from others, individuals can transform their internal narrative and nurture a more positive and empowering view of themselves. This shift in mindset is essential for building self-confidence and managing insecurities in healthier ways.

CULTIVATING SELF-COMPASSION AND KINDNESS TOWARD ONESELF

Individuals tend to be overly critical of themselves, constantly dwelling on their flaws and failures, which only exacerbates their feelings of insecurity. This negative self-talk can be detrimental to one's overall well-being, leading to decreased self-esteem and an inability to fully embrace oneself. Thus, it is imperative to develop self-compassion and kindness as important tools in combating insecurity. Self-compassion involves treating oneself with the same empathy, kindness, and understanding that one would extend to a close friend or loved one. This practice begins with acknowledging and accepting one's own imperfections and failures, rather than judging oneself harshly. By recognizing that all humans make mistakes and experience setbacks, individuals can cultivate a sense of common humanity, realizing that they are not alone in their struggles and insecurities. This realization helps to alleviate feelings of isolation, providing comfort and reassurance in knowing that everyone faces similar challenges in their journey toward self-acceptance. Self-compassion encourages individuals to practice self-care and prioritize their own well-being, both physically and emotionally. This includes engaging in activities that promote self-fulfillment and self-empowerment, such as engaging in hobbies, exercising, or seeking therapy when needed. By investing in oneself and consciously taking steps to meet one's needs, individuals demonstrate a commitment to their own growth and development, which can help to build their confidence and reduce feelings of insecurity. Alongside self-compassion, cultivating kindness toward oneself is equally important in overcoming in security. Kindness involves treating oneself with gentleness, forgiveness, and understanding, particularly during times of self-doubt or failure. Instead of berating oneself for perceived shortcomings, individuals can practice self-kindness by offering words of encouragement and support, just as they would to a friend experiencing similar struggles. This kind and understanding approach not only boosts one's self-esteem but also fosters resilience, allowing individuals to bounce back from setbacks and persevere in the face of adversity. Cultivating kindness toward oneself also involves embracing one's strengths and accomplishments, rather than dismissing them as insignificant. Insecure individuals tend to downplay their achievements or compare themselves unfavorably to others, further fueling their feelings of insecurity. By recognizing and celebrating their own unique qualities and accomplishments, individuals can develop a more positive self-image, bolstering their self-confidence and diminishing their insecurities. Cultivating self-compassion and kindness plays a vital role in overcoming insecurity. By practicing self-compassion, individuals can develop a sense of common humanity, recognizing that they are not alone in their struggles.

Self-compassion encourages individuals to prioritize their own well-being, investing in self-care and personal growth. Similarly, kindness toward oneself fosters resilience and self-esteem by replacing self-criticism with self-encouragement and celebrating one's strengths and accomplishments. By embracing self-compassion and kindness, individuals can break free from the cycle of insecurity, fostering a healthier relationship with them-

selves and ultimately leading to a more fulfilling and confident
life.

SILENCING NEGATIVE SELF-TALK AND REPLACING IT WITH POSITIVE AFFIRMATIONS

Negative self-talk refers to the internal dialogue in which individuals criticize and belittle themselves, leading to a cycle of low self-esteem and insecurity. This harmful self-talk often stems from past experiences, societal pressures, and comparison to others. It is essential to recognize that these negative beliefs are not based on facts but rather distorted perceptions of oneself. To combat negative self-talk, individuals should actively challenge and replace it with positive affirmations.

One effective technique to silence negative self-talk is to question the accuracy and validity of the negative thoughts. By challenging the negative beliefs, individuals can start to realize that they are not objective truths but mere interpretations. For example, if one frequently tells themselves, "I am not good enough," they can begin to question this belief by asking themselves, "What evidence do I have to support this statement? Are there situations where I have succeeded or felt confident?" Reflecting on achievements or positive experiences can provide a more balanced perspective and undermine the negative self-talk.Replacing negative self-talk with positive affirmations can help individuals reframe their mindset and build self-confidence. Positive affirmations are statements that reflect one's strengths, abilities, and worthiness. By repeating these affirmations regularly, individuals can internalize positive beliefs about themselves, which in turn improves self-esteem. For instance, replacing "I am not smart enough" with "I am intelligent and capable" can reshape one's perception and boost confidence. It is crucial to ensure that these positive affirmations are authentic and believable. Unrealistically positive affirmations may not resonate with individuals, making it harder to integrate them into their self-image. It is important to create affirmations that are specific, realistic, and tailored to one's personal journey. This may involve acknowledging personal growth, acknowledging strengths, or focusing on self-acceptance. In order to fully embrace positive affirmations and silence negative self-talk, individuals must cultivate an environment of self-compassion. Self-compassion involves treating oneself with kindness, understanding, and empathy. By practicing self-compassion, individuals can counteract the self-critical voice and develop a more nurturing relationship with themselves. This can be achieved through engaging in self-care activities, seeking support from loved ones, and practicing Mindfulness to cultivate self-aware ness and acceptance.

Silencing negative self-talk and replacing it with positive affirmations is a fundamental step towards overcoming insecurities. By challenging the accuracy of negative thoughts and replacing them with realistic and authentic affirmations, individuals can reshape their perception of themselves. Fostering an environment of self-compassion and cultivating self-awareness play crucial roles in maintaining positive self-talk. Overcoming insecurity requires ongoing effort and patience, but by actively replacing negative self-talk with positive affirmations, individuals can gradually build self-confidence and break free from the harmful cycle of low self-esteem.

BECOMING ONE'S OWN CHEERLEADER AND SOURCE OF ENCOURAGEMENT

This involves cultivating a positive and compassionate mindset towards oneself, celebrating personal achievements, and fostering inner confidence. Building self-esteem and self-worth is crucial, as it forms the foundation for embracing one's unique qualities and abilities, regardless of external validation. Becoming one's own cheerleader also means practicing self-compassion and having a supportive internal dialogue. Instead of being overly critical or judgmental, individuals should learn to acknowledge their efforts and recognize their strengths. This shift in mindset plays a significant role in overcoming insecurity. One key aspect of becoming one's own cheerleader is celebrating personal achievements. Oftentimes, individuals overlook their accomplishments or belittle their successes due to feelings of inadequacy. Acknowledging and celebrating achievements, no matter how small they may seem, is vital for building self-confidence. Whether it is completing a challenging task, receiving positive feedback, or achieving a personal goal, recognizing these accomplishments is a powerful way to counteract self-doubt. By taking the time to pat oneself on the back and relish in the sense of accomplishment, individuals can enhance their self-esteem and foster a positive self-image.

Another critical element of becoming one's own cheerleader is cultivating self-acceptance and embracing one's unique qualities and abilities. Insecurity often stems from comparing oneself to others and feeling inadequate or inferior. By recognizing and appreciating their individuality, individuals can develop a greater sense of self-worth. Each person possesses a unique set of talents, skills, and characteristics that contribute to their overall identity. By recognizing and embracing these attributes, individuals can gain a newfound appreciation for their own worth and value. Practicing self-compassion and maintaining a supportive internal dialogue are also crucial components of becoming one's own cheerleader. Many individuals engage in negative self-talk or harbor self-critical thoughts, which further perpetuate feelings of insecurity. Instead, it is important to offer oneself kindness, understanding, and encouragement. By adopting a compassionate mindset and speaking to oneself with self-assuredness and positivity, individuals can counteract insecurities and build a stronger sense of self-belief. This includes reframing negative thoughts into more constructive or empowering ones and challenging self-imposed limitations.

Overcoming insecurity requires individuals to become their own cheerleader and source of encouragement. This involves cultivating a positive and compassionate mindset, celebrating personal achievements, and embracing one's unique qualities and abilities. By building self-esteem and self-worth, individuals can gain the confidence to challenge and overcome their insecurities. Practicing self-com passion and maintaining a supportive internal dialogue are also vital for fostering inner confidence.

By becoming one's own cheerleader, individuals can develop a greater sense of self-belief and overcome the negative effects of insecurity. People often experience feelings of insecurity, especially during pivotal moments in their lives. Insecurities can be crippling, leading individuals to doubt their abilities, appearance, or worth. It is essential to acknowledge that insecurity is a common human experience and can be overcome by employing various strategies. One effective way to overcome insecurity is through self-reflection and self-acceptance. By taking the time to understand one's thoughts, feelings, and past experiences, individuals can gain a deeper understanding of their insecurities and the root causes behind them. This self-reflection allows for personal growth and can help individuals develop a sense of self-acceptance. Another key strategy in overcoming insecurity is by challenging negative self-talk and replacing it with positive affirmations. Negative self-talk often reinforces feelings of insecurity and self-doubt, perpetuating a cycle of negative thinking. By recognizing when negative thoughts arise and consciously reframing them, individuals can begin to shift their mindset and develop a more positive self-image. Seeking support from loved ones or a professional can be instrumental in overcoming insecurity. It is crucial to surround oneself with a supportive network of individuals who uplift and validate one's experiences. This can provide a sense of reassurance and help in building self-confidence. Seeking professional help, such as therapy or counseling, can provide a safe space for individuals to explore their insecurities and learn healthy coping mechanisms. Engaging in activities that promote personal growth and self-expression can also aid in overcoming insecurity. Engaging in activities such as journaling, painting, or engaging in physical exercise can help individuals channel their emotions and develop a stronger sense of self. Exploring new interests and hobbies can help in expanding one's comfort zone and building self-confidence. Another crucial aspect of overcoming insecurity is to practice self-care. Taking care of oneself physically, emotionally, and mentally is essential in building self-confidence and overcoming insecurity. Engaging in activities that promote relaxation, such as meditation or taking regular breaks, can help reduce stress levels and promote a sense of well-being. It is crucial to remember that overcoming insecurity is a journey that requires patience and self-compassion. It is essential to be gentle with oneself and not expect instant results. Embracing imperfections and embracing the learning process is vital in building resilience and overcoming insecurity in the long run. Insecurity is a common human experience, but it does not have to define one's life. By engaging in self-reflection, challenging negative self-talk, seeking support, engaging in personal growth activities, practicing self-care, and approaching the journey with patience and self-compassion, individuals can overcome insecurity and develop a stronger sense of self-confidence.

XIII. AVOIDING COMPARISONS

The act of comparing oneself to others often leads to feelings of inadequacy and self-doubt. When we constantly measure ourselves against others, we are setting ourselves up for disappointment and discontent. It is important to understand that everyone is unique, with their own strengths and weaknesses. Making comparisons disregards individuality and fails to accurately reflect the vast array of experiences, skills, and talents possessed by each individual. By avoiding comparisons, we allow ourselves the opportunity to focus on our own personal growth and development, rather than getting caught up in a never-ending cycle of competition. It is essential to remember that each person's journey is different, and we are all on our own path towards self-improvement. Comparisons can often be misleading and unrealistic. In today's highly curated social media culture, it is easy to fall into the trap of comparing oneself to carefully crafted online versions of others. These idealized portrayals often highlight only the best parts of someone's life, creating an illusion of perfection and happiness. It is important to remember that what we see online is not always an accurate reflection of reality. Comparing ourselves to the highlight reels of others only leads to feelings of inadequacy and the misconception that our lives are not as fulfilling or successful. It is crucial to maintain a healthy perspective and cultivate self-awareness, recognizing that everyone faces their own battles and struggles. Making comparisons can greatly hinder our own progress and self-esteem. When we constantly compare ourselves to others, we risk losing sight of our own achievements and successes. Instead of acknowledging our own growth, we belittle our accomplishments in light of someone else's achievements. This not only robs us of our own joy and sense of fulfillment but also prevents us from fully realizing our potential. By avoiding comparisons, we can focus on our own personal goals and aspirations, embracing our unique journey and celebrating our individual triumphs. Avoiding comparisons allows us to foster a healthier and more positive mindset. It enables us to shift our focus from external validation to internal fulfillment. When we stop seeking validation from others and comparing ourselves to their standards, we can cultivate self-acceptance and self-love. By embracing our individuality and celebrating our strengths, we can cultivate genuine confidence and overcome feelings of insecurity. It is in accepting and appreciating our own unique qualities that we can begin to build a solid foundation of self-worth and resilience. By avoiding comparisons, we empower ourselves to live authentically and joyfully, grounded in the belief that we are enough just as we are.

RECOGNIZING THE DANGERS OF COMPARING ONESELF TO OTHERS

It is natural for individuals to look at others and draw comparisons, but such actions can be detrimental to one's self-esteem and mental well-being. When we constantly compare ourselves to others, we place unrealistic expectations on ourselves and create a distorted perception of our own worth. In this digital age, social media platforms have provided a breeding ground for comparison, showcasing carefully curated versions of people's lives that can make us feel inadequate. We often only see the highlights and achievements of others, which can lead to a sense of failure and unworthiness. Comparing ourselves to others inhibits personal growth and hinders the development of our unique talents and abilities. Each individual possesses a unique set of skills and experiences, and by focusing on comparing ourselves to others, we diminish our own potential. It is crucial to acknowledge that everyone has their own journey, with varying goals, circumstances, and challenges. By comparing ourselves to others, we overlook our own achievements, strengths, and personal growth. Instead of using others as a benchmark for our own success, it is important to define our own measures of success and focus on personal growth and improvement. Comparing oneself to others breeds a toxic cycle of envy, resentment, and negativity. It becomes a constant battle of trying to keep up with others or feeling resentful toward those who seem to have more success or happiness. This negative mindset can drain our energy and hinder our ability to appreciate our own accomplishments and find contentment within ourselves. Recognizing the dangers of comparing oneself to others also includes understanding that everyone has their own struggles and insecurities. What may seem like a perfect life or effortless success on the surface may hide deep-rooted insecurities and personal challenges. Understanding this can help shift our mindset and foster empathy and compassion, not only for ourselves but also for others. Recognizing the dangers of comparing oneself to others is a crucial step in overcoming insecurity. It is natural to look at others for inspiration or guidance, but we should be mindful not to let these comparisons affect our self-esteem negatively. By focusing on our own personal growth, defining our own measures of success, and being compassionate towards ourselves and others, we can break free from the toxic cycle of comparison and cultivate a healthy and confident mindset. It is the journey of self-discovery and self-acceptance that leads to true fulfillment and confidence in one's own abilities.

APPRECIATING INDIVIDUAL STRENGTHS AND UNIQUE QUALITIES

It is important to recognize that each person has their own set of talents, skills, and attributes that make them truly unique. By understanding and valuing these individual strengths, individuals are able to build their self-esteem, embrace their authentic selves, and ultimately overcome their feelings of insecurity. Appreciating in dividual strengths involves acknowledging and celebrating one's own abilities and achievements. This can be accomplished by reflecting on past accomplishments, setting achievable goals, and recognizing personal growth. By acknowledging one's own successes, it becomes easier to believe in one's abilities and overcome feelings of insecurity. Appreciating individual strengths also entails recognizing and valuing the talents and abilities of others. By celebrating and supporting the unique qualities of others, individuals can create a positive and inclusive environment where everyone feels valued and accepted. Through genuine appreciation and admiration for the strengths of others, individuals can gain inspiration and motivation to develop their own skills and overcome their own insecurities.In addition to recognizing individual strengths, it is equally important to embrace and celebrate one's own unique qualities. Each person possesses a distinct combination of characteristics, experiences, and perspectives that contribute to their individuality. By embracing these unique qualities, individuals can cultivate a sense of self-acceptance and learn to appreciate their own worth. Embracing one's unique qualities involves accepting and loving oneself unconditionally, without comparing oneself to others. It requires an understanding that each person's journey is different and that there is no one-size-fits-all definition of success or happiness. By embracing their unique qualities, individuals can break free from the societal pressure to conform and begin to define their own version of success and happiness. Appreciating individual strengths and unique qualities also in volves recognizing that everyone has their own limitations and areas for growth. It is important to approach personal development with a sense of curiosity and a willingness to learn and improve. By embracing a growth mindset, individuals can overcome their insecurities by understanding that their worth is not solely defined by their shortcomings or failures, but rather by their willingness to learn and grow. This mindset allows individuals to see setbacks as opportunities for growth and development rather than reasons to feel insecure. In this way, appreciating individual strengths and unique qualities becomes an ongoing process of self-reflection and personal growth.

Appreciating individual strengths and unique qualities is instrumental in overcoming insecurity. By recognizing and valuing one's own abilities and achievements, individuals can build their self-esteem and believe in their own worth. By embracing and celebrating one's own unique qualities, individuals can cultivate a sense of self-acceptance and define their own version of success and happiness. By recognizing and appreciating the strengths and unique qualities of others, individuals can create a positive and inclusive environment where everyone feels valued and accepted. Through the appreciation of individual strengths and unique qualities, individuals can overcome insecurity and reach their full potential.

FOCUSING ON PERSONAL PROGRESS RATHER THAN EXTERNAL MARKERS OF SUCCESS

In today's society, external markers of success often dominate our perception of ourselves and others. We are constantly bombarded with messages that measure achievement based on material possessions, social status, or career accomplishments. This creates a toxic environment where our self-worth is tied to these external factors, leaving little room for personal growth or self-acceptance. It is important to realize that true success is not determined by these external markers, but rather by our own personal growth and happiness. By shifting our focus onto personal progress, we can break free from the cycle of insecurity and find fulfillment on our own terms.

Focusing on personal progress means valuing our individual journey and recognizing our own unique qualities and strengths. It requires us to define success for ourselves, rather than letting others dictate what it should look like. This can be a challenging endeavor, as it requires a deep level of self-reflection and introspection. We must take the time to identify our values, passions, and goals, and align our actions with these core principles. By doing so, we can create a sense of purpose and direction in our lives that is independent of external validation.

Focusing on personal progress allows us to embrace the process rather than fixating on the end result. Many times, our insecurity stems from comparing ourselves to others and feeling inadequate because we haven't achieved the same level of success or recognition. Success is not a destination, but rather a journey.

When we shift our mindset to view success as a continuous process of growth and improvement, we can find fulfillment in the small victories along the way. Each step, no matter how small, takes us closer to becoming the best version of ourselves.

In addition, focusing on personal progress enables us to cultivate a healthy relationship with failure. Insecurities often arise from a fear of failure and rejection. By reframing failure as an opportunity for learning and growth, we can overcome these fears and become more resilient. Instead of seeing failure as a reflection of our worth or abilities, we can view it as a stepping-stone towards success. Embracing failure as a natural part of the journey allows us to take risks and pursue our passions without fear of judgment or rejection.

Focusing on personal progress empowers us to take control of our own narrative and define our own sense of worth. By shifting our focus away from external markers of success, we can cultivate a healthier and more authentic sense of self. This process requires self-compassion, self-awareness, and a willingness to embrace vulnerability. It is not an easy path, but it is one that is essential for our personal growth and well-being. By focusing on personal progress, we can overcome insecurity and create a life that is truly fulfilling and meaningful.

In order to overcome insecurity, individuals must first recognize and acknowledge their insecurities. This self-awareness is essential for any personal growth journey, as it allows individuals to identify their triggers and understand the underlying reasons behind their insecurities. Secondly, individuals must practice self-compassion and forgiveness. It is important to remember that everyone has flaws and makes mistakes, and that it is not fair to hold oneself to impossible standards of perfection. By practicing self-compassion, individuals can learn to be kinder and more forgiving towards themselves, thus mitigating the negative impact of their insecurities. Surrounding oneself with a supportive network of family and friends can play a pivotal role in overcoming insecurity. Positive relationships can provide individuals with emotional support and reassurance, as well as serve as a sounding board for self-reflection and personal growth. It is important to be selective in choosing these relationships, and to prioritize quality over quantity. Building trust and open communication within these relationships is key, as it allows individuals to share their insecurities and receive feedback and validation in a safe and non-judgmental environment. Setting realistic and achievable goals can help individuals overcome insecurity. By setting small, manageable goals and celebrating each achievement, individuals can gradually increase their confidence and self-esteem. This incremental approach allows individuals to take measured risks and challenge their insecurities, ultimately leading to personal growth and empowerment. Seeking professional help, such as therapy or counseling, can provide individuals with the tools and support necessary to overcome deep-rooted insecurities. Licensed professionals can help individuals explore the underlying causes of their insecurities, develop coping mechanisms, and work towards building a healthier self-image. They can also provide guidance in implementing effective strategies to manage and overcome insecurity in daily life. Practicing self-care is crucial in overcoming insecurity. Engaging in activities that promote mental, physical, and emotional well-being can significantly improve self-esteem and outlook on life. This can include activities such as exercise, meditation, journaling, or engaging in hobbies and interests. Taking care of oneself not only boosts confidence and self-worth, but also demonstrates a commitment to one's own personal growth and happiness. Overcoming insecurity is a multifaceted process that requires self-awareness, self-compassion, a supportive network, realistic goal-setting, seeking professional help, and practicing self-care. It is important to approach this journey with patience and understanding, as personal growth takes time and effort. By implementing these strategies, individuals can overcome their insecurities and develop a stronger sense of self-worth and confidence.

XIV. PRACTICING MINDFULNESS

Practicing Mindfulness is a powerful tool that can help individuals overcome insecurity. Mindfulness involves being fully present in the moment, without judgment or attachment to thoughts or emotions. By cultivating a nonjudgmental awareness of their thoughts and emotions, individuals can gain insight into the patterns of their insecure thoughts and begin to challenge them. Through Mindfulness, individuals can develop a greater sense of self-acceptance, relinquishing the need for external validation and finding true confidence within themselves. Mindfulness allows individuals to develop a deep understanding of their emotions, helping them to address and manage insecurity directly. By observing their emotions without judgment, individuals can become more attuned to the triggers and underlying beliefs that contribute to their insecurity, allowing them to respond to these feelings with compassion and understanding. Mindfulness can help individuals to cultivate a greater sense of gratitude and appreciation for themselves and their accomplishments, which can serve as a powerful antidote to feelings of insecurity. By practicing gratitude and focusing on the positive aspects of their life, individuals can start to shift their perspective from one of comparison and self-criticism to one of self-acceptance and self-love. Mindfulness can also contribute to increased self-awareness, allowing individuals to become aware of the negative self-talk and limiting beliefs that often underlie feelings of insecurity. By observing and challenging these thoughts, individuals can work towards replacing them with more positive and empowering ones. Mindfulness can be practiced through various techniques, such as meditation, deep breathing exercises, and body scans. These techniques can help individuals to anchor themselves in the present moment and develop a heightened sense of self-awareness. Engaging in regular Mindfulness practices can also help individuals to cultivate a greater sense of resilience and adaptability, enabling them to navigate the inevitable setbacks and challenges that life presents with greater ease and confidence. Mindfulness can serve as a powerful tool for managing stress, as it encourages individuals to slow down, breathe, and focus on the present moment, rather than getting caught up in worries and fears about the future. Practicing Mindfulness can be an invaluable tool for overcoming insecurity. By cultivating a nonjudgmental awareness of their thoughts and emotions, individuals can gain insight into their patterns of insecure thinking and develop a greater sense of self-acceptance. Mindfulness also allows individuals to address and manage their emotions directly, cultivating a sense of compassion and understanding towards themselves. Mindfulness can help individuals to cultivate gratitude and appreciation for themselves and their accomplishments, shifting their perspective from one of comparison and self-criticism to one of self-acceptance and self-love. By challenging negative thoughts and limiting beliefs, individuals can work towards replacing them with more positive and empowering ones. The regular practice of Mindfulness techniques can contribute to increased self-awareness, resilience, adaptability, and stress management, all of which are essential for overcoming insecurity and cultivating true confidence.

BEING PRESENT AND OBSERVANT OF ONE'S THOUGHTS AND EMOTIONS

Insecurity often arises from a lack of self-awareness and an inability to acknowledge and understand one's own thoughts and emotions. By practicing Mindfulness and being fully present in the moment, individuals can develop a deeper understanding of themselves and their insecurities. This requires actively observing and reflecting upon one's thoughts and emotions without judgment or attachment. By simply observing these internal states, individuals can gain valuable insights into the root causes of their insecurities. For example, someone may notice that they feel insecure when they receive criticism from others. Through observation, they may realize that this insecurity stems from a deep-seated fear of rejection or a desire for approval. Once individuals become aware of these underlying issues, they can begin to address and overcome them. In addition to gaining insight, being present and observant also allows individuals to respond to their insecurities in a more constructive manner. When insecure thoughts or emotions arise, individuals can choose to acknowledge them without becoming overwhelmed or controlled by them. Instead of reacting impulsively or defensively, individuals can take a step back, observe their internal state, and respond with compassion and understanding. By being present with their insecurities, individuals can develop a sense of acceptance and self-compassion, which is essential for healing and growth. Being observant of one's thoughts and emotions can help individuals differentiate between rational and irrational insecurities. In many cases, insecurities are based on distorted beliefs or negative self-perceptions. By actively observing these thoughts and emotions, individuals can challenge and reframe them. For example, someone who feels insecure about their physical appearance may observe their negative self-talk, such as "I'm ugly" or "Nobody will ever find me attractive." Through observation, they can recognize these thoughts as irrational and replace them with more realistic and positive beliefs. This process allows individuals to cultivate a healthier self-image and reduce the impact of their insecurities. Being present and observant of one's thoughts and emotions can also provide individuals with a sense of empowerment and control. Insecurity often causes individuals to feel overwhelmed and powerless, as if their emotions and thoughts are running their lives. By developing the skill of observation, individuals can take an active role in their own emotional well-being. They can choose to cultivate positive thoughts and redirect negative emotions, rather than being at the mercy of their insecurities. This sense of agency can be incredibly empowering and can lead to significant personal growth and development. Being present and observant of one's thoughts and emotions is a powerful tool for overcoming insecurity. Through observation, individuals can gain insight into the root causes of their insecurities, respond to them in a more constructive manner, differentiate between rational and irrational thoughts, cultivate self-compassion, and empower themselves to take control of their emotional well-being. By cultivating this skill, individuals can embark on a journey of self-discovery and healing, ultimately leading to greater self-confidence and a more fulfilling life.

DETACHING FROM NEGATIVE THOUGHTS AND REFRAMING THEM POSITIVELY

Negative thoughts have a powerful impact on our self-esteem and contribute to feelings of insecurity. By detaching ourselves from these negative thoughts, we can regain control over our own perception. One effective technique for doing so is by reframing negative thoughts in a positive light. For example, instead of dwelling on past failures or perceived inadequacies, we can choose to focus on our strengths and previous successes. This shift in perspective allows us to see ourselves in a more positive and empowering way. Practicing self-compassion is crucial in the process of detaching from negative thoughts. We must learn to treat ourselves with kindness, understanding, and empathy, just as we would treat a loved one. This involves acknowledging and accepting our flaws and imperfections, understanding that they do not define us as individuals. By adopting a mindset of self-compassion, we are able to challenge negative thoughts and replace them with more constructive and uplifting ones. Another strategy for detaching from negative thoughts is by practicing Mindfulness. Mindfulness involves being fully present and aware of our thoughts, feelings, and sensations in the present moment, without judgment or attachment. By observing our negative thoughts from a distance, we can gradually detach ourselves from them, recognizing that they are not a reflection of our true selves. Through regular practice, Mindfulness trains our minds to focus on the present moment rather than getting caught up in destructive thought patterns. In addition to Mindfulness, cognitive-behavioral therapy (CBT) is a widely used therapeutic approach that helps individuals challenge and reframe negative thoughts. This type of therapy focuses on recognizing and altering negative thought patterns that contribute to insecurity and low self-esteem. By identifying distortions in our thinking and replacing them with more rational and positive thoughts, we can gradually shift our perspective and enhance our self-image. Seeking support from others can be instrumental in detaching from negative thoughts and reframing them positively. Whether through joining support groups, confiding in trusted friends or family members, or seeking guidance from a professional counselor, sharing our struggles and insecurities with others can provide valuable insights and alternative perspectives. It can remind us that we are not alone in our experience and that there are individuals who care and understand. Detaching from negative thoughts and reframing them positively is an essential aspect of overcoming insecurity and developing a healthier self-perception. By challenging negative thoughts, practicing self-compassion, Mindfulness, and seeking support from others, we can break free from the damaging effects of insecurity and cultivate a more positive and resilient mindset. Although it may require time and effort, the process of detaching from negative thoughts is a transformative journey that enables individuals to embrace their true worth and fulfill their potential.

ENGAGING IN MEDITATION OR MINDFULNESS EXERCISES TO CULTIVATE SELF-AWARENESS

Cultivating self-awareness is a powerful tool for overcoming insecurity, and one effective way to achieve this is by engaging in meditation or Mindfulness exercises. Meditation is a practice that has been utilized for centuries across various cultures and belief systems, and it involves training the mind to focus and redirect thoughts. By dedicating time to quiet contemplation, individuals can observe their thoughts, feelings, and physical sensations without judgment or attachment. Through meditation, individuals can develop a heightened sense of self-awareness as they become more attuned to their inner experiences and thought patterns. This increased self-awareness allows individuals to recognize and challenge their insecurities, without becoming overwhelmed by them. Meditation helps individuals develop a sense of presence in the current moment, which can be particularly beneficial for addressing feelings of insecurity. Rather than allowing negative thoughts or fears about the future to consume their attention, individuals can learn to anchor themselves in the present moment through Mindfulness exercises. Mindfulness involves intentionally focusing attention on the present moment, without judgment. This practice helps individuals shift their focus away from self-doubt and insecurity, promoting a greater sense of calm and acceptance. By engaging in Mindfulness exercises, individuals can learn to observe their insecurities with curiosity and compassion, rather than being overcome by them. Cultivating self-awareness through meditation and Mindfulness can provide individuals with a clearer understanding of their values, priorities, and strengths. Insecurity often arises from a lack of self-confidence or a misalignment between personal values and societal expectations. By embarking on a journey of self-discovery, individuals can gain insight into their true selves, free from the influence of external pressures. This self-understanding allows individuals to become more secure in their own identities and choices, recognizing that they are unique and valuable. Self-awareness fosters a greater sense of empowerment and personal agency, as individuals become more attuned to their own desires and needs. This heightened self-awareness equips individuals with the knowledge and confidence to stand up for themselves, assert their boundaries, and pursue their goals, ultimately reducing feelings of insecurity. To conclude, engaging in meditation or Mindfulness exercises is an effective means of cultivating self-awareness and overcoming insecurity. Through these practices, individuals can observe their thoughts, feelings, and physical sensations without judgment, leading to a greater understanding and acceptance of oneself. Meditation and Mindfulness also promote presence in the current moment, allowing individuals to detach from negative thoughts and fears about the future. By developing a clearer sense of values and priorities, individuals can address the root causes of their insecurities and align their actions and beliefs accordingly. Self-awareness equips individuals with the confidence and empowerment necessary to confront and overcome their insecurities, leading to a more secure and fulfilling life.

One of the most effective ways to overcome insecurity is by practicing self-compassion. Insecurity often stems from a deep-rooted belief that we are not good enough or deserving of love and validation. This negative self-perception can greatly impact our overall well-being and prevent us from achieving our full potential. Self-compassion offers an alternative perspective that can help us break free from the shackles of insecurity. Self-compassion involves treating ourselves with kindness, understanding, and acceptance, just as we would treat a close friend or loved one. It is about acknowledging our imperfections and mistakes with a sense of empathy and embracing ourselves as flawed but deserving individuals. By cultivating self-compassion, we can learn to counteract the negative self-talk that often accompanies feelings of insecurity. Instead of criticizing and berating ourselves for our perceived shortcomings, we can choose to offer ourselves words of encouragement and support. This shift in mindset can have a profound impact on our self-esteem and self-worth, helping us to feel more secure in ourselves and our abilities. Self-compassion allows us to recognize that everyone experiences insecurities and struggles at times, and this does not make us any less worthy or valuable. It reminds us that we are all imperfect humans on a journey of growth and learning. Rather than comparing ourselves unfavorably to others, self-compassion encourages us to focus on our own unique strengths and accomplishments. It teaches us to celebrate our successes, no matter how small, and to value ourselves for who we are, rather than basing our self-worth on external validation. Another key aspect of self-compassion is the ability to practice self-forgiveness. Insecurities often arise from past mistakes and failures that we continue to blame ourselves for. By offering ourselves forgiveness and letting go of the burden of guilt, we can begin to heal the wounds caused by insecurity. Through self-compassion, we come to understand that making mistakes is a natural part of life and that they do not define our worth as individuals. Instead of dwelling on our past shortcomings, we can choose to learn from them and grow into stronger and more resilient individuals. Self-compassion encourages us to prioritize self-care and self-nurturing. By taking care of our physical, emotional, and mental well-being, we send a powerful message to ourselves that we are deserving of love, compassion, and respect. This can involve engaging in activities that bring us joy, practicing Mindfulness and relaxation techniques, seeking support from trusted friends or professionals, and setting boundaries in our relationships. When we make self-care a priority, we show ourselves that we are worthy of investing time and energy into, further strengthening our sense of security and self-worth. Self-compassion is a powerful tool for overcoming insecurity. By treating ourselves with kindness, acceptance, and forgiveness, we can challenge the negative self-perceptions that contribute to insecurity and cultivate a stronger sense of self-worth. Through self-compassion, we can learn to embrace our imperfections, celebrate our strengths, and prioritize our overall well-being. It is an ongoing practice that can lead to transformative growth and help us break free from the grip of insecurity.

XV. EMBRACING FAILURE AS LEARNING OPPORTUNITIES

Often times, individuals who struggle with insecurity tend to view failures as confirmation of their self-doubt and inadequacy. Reframing failure can be transformative and empowering. Embracing failure as a learning opportunity allows individuals to grow and develop from their mistakes rather than being held back by them. By shifting one's perspective, failure becomes an integral part of the journey towards success and self-growth. To begin with, embracing failure as learning opportunities enables individuals to develop resilience and perseverance. Failure is an inevitable part of life, and by recognizing its potential for growth and learning, individuals can bounce back from setbacks with renewed determination. Instead of being discouraged by failure, individuals can use it as a motivating force to keep pushing forward and striving for their goals. By viewing failure as a steppingstone to success rather than an indication of personal shortcomings, individuals can develop the resilience needed to overcome obstacles and conquer their insecurities. Embracing failure as learning opportunities allows individuals to identify their weaknesses and areas for improvement. Failure provides valuable feedback that can help individuals understand what went wrong and how they can do better in the future. Whether it is in academics, work, or personal relationships, failure can offer insights into specific areas that require attention and growth. By analyzing the reasons behind failure, individuals can identify patterns, habits, or behaviors that need to be addressed for future success. This process of introspection and self-reflection not only fosters personal growth but also helps individuals overcome their insecurities by confronting and addressing them head-on. Embracing failure as learning opportunities cultivates a growth mindset. The concept of a growth mindset, popularized by psychologist Carol S. Dweck, suggests that individuals who believe their abilities can be developed through dedication and hard work are more likely to achieve success. By adopting a growth mindset, individuals view failure not as a reflection of their inherent limitations but as an opportunity for growth and improvement. This mindset shift allows individuals to view challenges as chances for personal development and to approach them with enthusiasm rather than fear. The belief that one's abilities are not fixed, but rather malleable, empowers individuals to constantly strive for improvement and overcome their insecurities. Embracing failure as learning opportunities is crucial in overcoming insecurity. By reframing failure as a chance for growth, individuals can develop resilience, identify areas for improvement, and cultivate a growth mindset. Rather than being held back by fears of failure, individuals can view setbacks as steppingstones towards success. Through self-reflection and a dedication to personal growth, individuals can not only overcome their insecurities but also thrive in the face of failure. By embracing failure as part of the learning process, individuals can unlock their true potential and achieve lasting success.

CHANGING PERSPECTIVE ON FAILURES AS SETBACKS TO OPPORTUNITIES

Traditionally, failures have been seen as setbacks, moments of defeat that lower one's self-esteem and confidence. A college-level understanding acknowledges that failures can be transformed into opportunities for growth and self-improvement. This shift in perspective is not only empowering but also essential for personal development and success. Firstly, failures provide valuable lessons that cannot be learned through success alone. When we experience failure, we are forced to reassess our strategies, reconsider our choices, and identify areas in need of improvement. This reflective process allows us to gain invaluable insights into our strengths and weaknesses, ultimately leading to growth and self-discovery. Through failure, we acquire knowledge that can be applied to future endeavors, increasing our chances of success. In this way, failure becomes a steppingstone towards greater achievements rather than a roadblock. Failures can build resilience and mental strength. When we encounter setbacks, we are confronted with challenges that test our ability to persevere and bounce back. Embracing failures as opportunities allows us to develop resilience, enabling us to handle adversity with grace and determination. This ability is particularly vital in college life, as students often face numerous obstacles, whether it be academic struggles, personal setbacks, or failed relationships. By harnessing failures as steppingstones, college students can cultivate the mindset and emotional fortitude necessary to face challenges effectively, ensuring personal growth and success. Changing our perspective on failures promotes growth mindset and fosters innovation. Embracing failure requires us to adopt a growth mindset, one that sees potential and opportunity in every setback. When we understand that failure is not a reflection of our worth but rather a temporary setback, we become more willing to take risks and pursue innovative ideas. This mindset is invaluable in a college setting, where encouraging creativity and exploration is paramount to personal and intellectual development. Failure ceases to be a source of anxiety or shame but rather a necessary and expected part of the learning process, propelling us towards new discoveries and breakthroughs. By embracing failures as opportunities, we cultivate a positive mindset and foster self-com passion. Instead of dwelling on our mistakes and harboring negative self-talk, we approach failures with kindness and understanding. This shift in perspective allows us to engage in constructive self-reflection and acknowledge that failures do not define us as individuals. College students, in particular, may feel burdened by the overwhelming expectations placed upon them. By changing their perspective on failures, they can alleviate the self-imposed pressure and prioritize personal growth and well-being over external validation. Changing our perspective on failures from setbacks to opportunities is crucial for overcoming insecurities and achieving personal growth. Failures provide valuable lessons, build resilience, foster innovation, and promote a positive mindset. By embracing failures, college students can navigate the challenges of higher education with confidence and grace, ultimately shaping their own path to success.

ANALYZING FAILURES FOR LESSONS AND AREAS OF IMPROVEMENT

When individuals experience failure, they often feel a sense of disappointment and doubt in their own abilities. By reframing failure as an opportunity for growth, one can gain valuable insights and identify areas for improvement. In order to effectively analyze failures, it is important to adopt a reflective mindset and ask critical questions. Firstly, one should evaluate the factors that contributed to the failure. Was it a lack of preparation, misguided strategies, or unforeseen circumstances? By identifying these factors, individuals can determine the root causes of their failures and devise strategies to overcome them in the future. It is crucial to assess one's own behaviors and decision-making processes. Were there any patterns of self-sabotage or limiting beliefs that hindered success? Recognizing these patterns enables individuals to work on their mindset and develop healthier habits. Analyzing failures provides an opportunity to gain valuable lessons. Failures often reveal weaknesses and blind spots that may have been overlooked during times of success. By acknowledging and learning from these lessons, individuals can strengthen their skillsets and become more resilient in the face of adversity. Analyzing failures can lead to areas of improvement. It allows individuals to identify specific skills or knowledge gaps that need to be addressed. For instance, if a student fails a math test, they can recognize that they need to study certain topics more thoroughly or seek help from a tutor. This process of self-reflection helps individuals set realistic goals and develop personalized action plans for improvement. Analyzing failures promotes a growth mindset. Instead of being consumed by self-doubt, individuals can view failures as temporary setbacks on the path to success. This mindset shift enables individuals to maintain perseverance and motivation in the face of challenges. They understand that failure does not define their capabilities, but rather serves as a steppingstone towards personal growth. Analyzing failures fosters a sense of accountability. By taking responsibility for one's own actions and outcomes, individuals can gain control over their lives and actively work towards improvement. This accountability empowers individuals to make proactive choices that align with their goals and values. Analyzing failures for lessons and areas of improvement is a crucial step towards overcoming insecurity. By reframing failure as an opportunity for growth, individuals can gain valuable insights and identify areas for improvement. This process involves evaluating the factors that contributed to the failure, assessing one's behaviors and decision-making processes, learning from the lessons revealed by failure, identifying areas for improvement, fostering a growth mindset, and cultivating accountability. Through this process, individuals can develop resilience, enhance their skillsets, and work towards achieving their goals with confidence.

RECOGNIZING THAT FAILURE IS A NATURAL PART OF GROWTH AND SUCCESS

Sometimes, insecurity stems from a fear of making mistakes or falling short of expectations. It is important to realize that failure is not something to be feared but rather embraced as a steppingstone towards growth and success. Throughout history, countless successful individuals have encountered multiple failures before achieving greatness. For instance, Thomas Edison failed over a thousand times before inventing the practical electric light bulb. His relentless efforts and resilience in the face of failure ultimately led to his groundbreaking success. Likewise, J.K. Rowling faced numerous rejections from publishers before her Harry Potter series became a worldwide phenomenon. These examples highlight the fact that failure is not indicative of one's worth or potential, but rather an opportunity to learn, adapt, and ultimately succeed. Acknowledging that failure is a natural part of life also helps to alleviate insecurity by shifting one's mindset. Instead of viewing failures as personal shortcomings, it is important to perceive them as valuable learning experiences. Every failure presents an opportunity to reevaluate one's approach, adjust strategies, and improve upon previous attempts. This growth mindset fosters resilience, self-confidence, and a belief that setbacks are not permanent obstacles but rather temporary setbacks. Embracing failure as an integral part of the journey towards success allows individuals to persevere, take risks, and ultimately surpass their insecurities. Recognizing that failure is a shared experience amongst all individuals can also help in overcoming insecurity. It is easy to believe that failures are isolated incidents unique to oneself, leading to feelings of inadequacy and self-doubt. Understanding that even the most accomplished individuals have encountered failure can shatter this notion. . Failure is a universal experience that unites individuals from all walks of life. By acknowledging this shared aspect of human existence, individuals can gain a sense of solace and realize that their insecurities are not unique or insurmountable. This collective understanding allows for a sense of community and support, fostering personal growth and the development of resilience.

Recognizing that failure is a natural part of growth and success is crucial in overcoming insecurity. By viewing failures as learning experiences rather than personal shortcomings, individuals can develop a growth mindset, resilience, and self-confidence. The successes of countless individuals throughout history serve as proof that failure is not an indicator of worth or potential. Understanding that failure is a shared experience amongst all individuals can help in shattering feelings of isolation and inadequacy. Embracing failure as an opportunity for growth not only allows individuals to surpass their insecurities but also paves the way for personal and professional success.

In order to overcome insecurity, it is essential to first understand its origins and underlying causes. Insecurity can stem from various sources, such as past experiences, societal pressures, and self-imposed standards. One major factor that contributes to insecurity is the comparison trap. In a society driven by social media and unrealistic standards of beauty, it is easy to feel inadequate when constantly comparing oneself to others. The relentless pursuit of perfection, fueled by the fear of being judged or rejected, further exacerbates feelings of insecurity. Past experiences, such as childhood trauma or negative relationships, can deeply impact one's sense of self-worth and contribute to a perpetual cycle of insecurity. These experiences often create a distorted self-image, making it challenging to see oneself in a positive light. Societal pressures, such as gender expectations or cultural norms, can breed insecurity by imposing rigid standards that individuals feel compelled to meet. The fear of not measuring up to these expectations can weigh heavily on one's self-esteem and confidence. Another common cause of insecurity is the fear of failure. This fear can paralyze individuals, preventing them from taking risks, pursuing their goals, or embracing new opportunities. The constant worry of not being good enough or making mistakes can undermine one's self-belief, leading to persistent insecurity.

To overcome insecurity, it is crucial to cultivate self-compassion and develop a healthy self-image. This involves recognizing and challenging negative self-talk and replacing it with positive affirmations. By reframing negative thoughts and embracing self-acceptance, individuals can start to dismantle the foundations of insecurity. Seeking support from trusted friends, family members, or therapists can also be instrumental in this process. Talking openly about insecurities and receiving reassurance and guidance from others can provide the necessary perspective and encouragement needed to overcome them.

Building self-confidence is another essential step in overcoming insecurity. Engaging in activities or hobbies that bring joy and a sense of accomplishment can boost self-esteem. Surrounding oneself with positive influences and supportive individuals can further contribute to building confidence. Setting realistic goals and celebrating small victories along the way can help individuals recognize their strengths and talents. By focusing on personal growth rather than external validation, individuals can develop a strong sense of self-assurance.

Addressing the fear of failure is also crucial in overcoming insecurity. It is important to understand that failure is a natural part of life, and it does not define one's worth or capabilities. Embracing failure as an opportunity for growth and learning can transform one's perspective, allowing them to approach challenges with resilience and a growth mindset. Developing effective coping mechanisms, such as Mindfulness techniques or journaling, can also help manage the fear of failure and provide a sense of clarity and perspective. Overcoming insecurity requires a multifaceted approach that involves understanding its underlying causes, cultivating self-compassion, building self-confidence, and addressing the fear of failure. By challenging negative thoughts, seeking support, and focusing on personal growth, individuals can gradually overcome insecurity and cultivate a positive and healthy self-image. The journey towards overcoming insecurity may be challenging, but with perseverance, self-reflection, and support, individuals can break free from the chains of insecurity and embrace a life filled with self-assurance and genuine happiness.

XVI. WORKING ON EMOTIONAL INTELLIGENCE

Emotional intelligence plays a pivotal role in overcoming insecurity. It involves the ability to understand and manage one's emotions effectively, as well as accurately perceive and navigate the feelings of others in interpersonal relationships. Developing emotional intelligence starts with self-awareness – being aware of one's emotions, thoughts, and behaviors. This awareness allows individuals to recognize when they are feeling insecure and why. By identifying the triggers and underlying thoughts associated with insecurity, individuals can begin to challenge and reframe their negative beliefs. This process of self-reflection and introspection allows individuals to gain a deeper understanding of their insecurities and develop strategies to address them. In addition to self-awareness, emotional intelligence also encompasses self-regulation. This involves the ability to manage and control one's emotions, especially in situations that may trigger insecurity. By practicing self-regulation, individuals can avoid impulsive behavior and instead respond to situations in a more rational and constructive manner. This skill allows individuals to effectively handle and navigate challenging situations that may exacerbate feelings of insecurity.

Another crucial aspect of emotional intelligence is empathy. Empathy involves understanding and sharing the emotions of others, which can be particularly helpful in overcoming insecurity. By empathizing with others, individuals are able to broaden their perspective and gain a better understanding of the diverse experiences and emotions of people around them. This understanding can help individuals overcome their own insecurities by realizing that others have similar struggles and that their insecurities are not unique. Social skills play a significant role in developing emotional intelligence. Building and maintaining positive relationships are essential for overcoming insecurity. Effective communication, active listening, and conflict resolution skills are all vital components of social skills. By improving these skills, individuals can develop stronger relationships and create a supportive network that can help them address and overcome their insecurities. Surrounding oneself with positive and supportive individuals can enhance self-esteem and provide guidance and reassurance during times of insecurity.

Cultivating emotional intelligence requires continuous practice and self-reflection. It involves being aware of one's emotions, regulating them, empathizing with others, and developing effective social skills. Emotionally intelligent individuals are more likely to recognize and address their insecurities, rather than allowing them to become overwhelming and detrimental to their well-being. By consciously working on emotional intelligence, individuals can gain a better understanding of themselves and others, which ultimately helps them overcome their insecurities and live a more fulfilling and confident life.

Emotional intelligence is a vital skill that can aid in overcoming insecurity. Through self-awareness, self-regulation, empathy, and social skills, individuals can gain a deeper understanding of their insecurities and develop strategies to address them. By honing their emotional intelligence, individuals can navigate challenging situations with more confidence, build stronger relationships, and ultimately overcome their insecurities. Working on emotional intelligence is a lifelong journey, but the rewards of increased self-confidence and personal growth are worth the effort.

DEVELOPING SELF-AWARENESS OF EMOTIONS AND HOW THEY INFLUENCE ACTIONS

Individuals struggling with insecurity may not fully understand the root of their emotional responses, leading to a cycle of negative thoughts and behaviors. Self-awareness, on the other hand, allows individuals to recognize and acknowledge their emotions, providing an opportunity to understand how these influences affect their actions. By gaining insight into the connection between emotions and actions, individuals can begin to develop healthier coping mechanisms to overcome their insecurities. Emotions play a fundamental role in shaping our behavior. They can drive us to act in ways that either benefit or hinder our personal growth and relationships. Developing self-awareness involves the process of observing and understanding our emotions, the triggers that lead to them, and the subsequent actions they prompt. For example, an individual struggling with insecurity may often feel a sense of self-doubt and unworthiness in social situations. These emotions can be triggered by events such as receiving criticism or perceiving others as more successful. Without self-awareness, such individuals may respond to these emotions by withdrawing from social interactions or avoiding situations that make them feel vulnerable. Through self-awareness, they can recognize that their emotions stem from their insecurities and understand the negative impact their actions have on their well-being.

Self-awareness also allows individuals to gain a deeper understanding of the underlying causes of their insecurities. In many cases, past experiences or traumas contribute to feelings of inadequacy and self-doubt. By recognizing and exploring these root causes, individuals can begin to address and heal from them. For instance, someone who experienced bullying during their childhood may carry feelings of shame and inferiority into adulthood. Through self-awareness, they can identify the connection between their past experiences and their current insecurities. This understanding empowers them to seek therapy or engage in self-reflection exercises to challenge and reframe their negative beliefs. Self-awareness enables individuals to recognize patterns in their emotional responses and behaviors. This insight allows them to preemptively address and modify maladaptive coping mechanisms. For example, an individual struggling with insecurity may have a tendency to seek constant validation from others. Self-awareness helps them recognize this pattern and understand how it perpetuates their insecurities, as they become reliant on external affirmations for self-worth. Armed with this knowledge, they can begin to cultivate self-compassion, practice positive self-talk, and rely on their own internal validation to break free from the cycle.

Developing self-awareness of emotions and how they influence actions is crucial for overcoming insecurity. It allows individuals to recognize and understand the connection between their emotions and behaviors, providing an opportunity to develop healthier coping mechanisms. By gaining insight into the root causes of their insecurities, individuals can address and heal from past traumas. Self-awareness helps individuals recognize patterns in their emotional responses and behaviors, empowering them to proactively modify maladaptive coping mechanisms. Self-awareness serves as the foundation for personal

growth, helping individuals navigate their insecurities with resilience and compassion.

PRACTICING EMPATHY AND UNDERSTANDING TOWARDS OTHERS

Practicing empathy and understanding towards others is a crucial aspect of overcoming insecurity. Insecurities often stem from a self-centered perspective, where individuals become overly concerned with how others perceive them. By shifting the focus away from oneself and towards others, individuals can gain a deeper understanding of the diverse range of experiences and emotions that people go through. Empathy, the ability to understand and share the feelings of others, allows individuals to put themselves in someone else's shoes, breaking down barriers and fostering meaningful connections. This practice requires active listening and open-mindedness, as it is important to validate and respect others' perspectives, even if they may differ from our own. When individuals make a conscious effort to understand others, it not only helps them gain perspective and enhance their own emotional intelligence, but it also creates an environment of trust and support. By practicing empathy and understanding, individuals can help build a more inclusive and compassionate society. Practicing empathy and understanding towards others also helps in developing stronger and healthier relationships. Insecurity often leads to a fear of rejection or judgment, causing individuals to put up walls and distance themselves from others. By actively listening and seeking to understand others' experiences, individuals can break down these barriers and create more meaningful connections. When we take the time to understand others, we are more likely to respond in a considerate and thoughtful manner. This sense of understanding fosters a sense of trust and respect, allowing relationships to flourish and grow. Practicing empathy and understanding also promotes effective communication, as individuals feel comfortable expressing their thoughts and emotions without fear of judgment or consequences. In doing so, individuals can build stronger support systems and develop more fulfilling relationships. Practicing empathy and understanding aids in personal growth and self-acceptance. In securities often stem from a lack of self-confidence and self-worth, causing individuals to constantly seek validation from others. When individuals shift their focus towards understanding and empathizing with others, they become less fixated on their own insecurities. By witnessing and acknowledging the struggles and challenges that others face, individuals can gain a broader perspective on their own experiences and learning to appreciate their unique strengths and weaknesses. This practice helps foster self-acceptance and self-compassion, as individuals begin to recognize that everyone has their own insecurities and that it is a normal part of the human experience. With this newfound understanding, individuals can strive for personal growth, focusing on their own development and journey rather than constantly comparing themselves to others. By practicing empathy and understanding, individuals can cultivate a sense of self-awareness and self-acceptance that ultimately leads to greater confidence and security. Practicing empathy and understanding towards others is essential in overcoming insecurity. Through active listening, open-mindedness, and a genuine desire to understand others, individuals can break down barriers, foster meaningful connections, and develop stronger and healthier relationships. This practice also aids in personal growth and self-acceptance, as individuals gain a broader perspective on their own experiences and learn to appreciate their unique strengths and weaknesses. By practicing empathy and under-standing, individuals can build a more inclusive and compas-sionate society, free from the constraints of insecurity.

LEARNING TO REGULATE EMOTIONS EFFECTIVELY AND ASSERTIVELY

This is a crucial step in overcoming insecurity. Insecurity often arises from a lack of self-confidence and the fear of being judged by others. It is essential to develop strategies to regulate emotions effectively in order to regain control over one's mind and reduce feelings of insecurity. One effective technique is Mindfulness meditation, which involves focusing one's attention on the present moment without judgment. By practicing Mindfulness, individuals can become more aware of their emotions and learn to control their reactions to them. This allows them to approach their insecurities with a sense of curiosity and compassion, rather than being overwhelmed by them. Assertiveness training can help individuals express their needs and desires in a confident and considerate manner, thus reducing feelings of insecurity. Assertiveness involves communicating effectively, setting boundaries, and standing up for oneself without resorting to passive or aggressive behavior. By learning assertiveness skills, individuals can gain a sense of self-worth and feel more secure in their interactions with others. Understanding and managing one's emotions is fundamental to building healthy relationships. Insecurity can often lead to negative assumptions and interpretations of others' behavior, which can strain relationships and further reinforce feelings of insecurity. By learning to regulate emotions effectively, individuals can prevent these negative thought patterns from taking control and approach relationships with a clearer and more positive mindset. The ability to regulate emotions effectively can also contribute to better problem-solving skills. Insecurity often hinders individuals in making rational decisions as they might be overly influenced by negative emotions or fear of failure. By learning to regulate emotions, individuals can approach challenges with a more balanced and rational mindset, enabling them to come up with more effective problem-solving strategies. Learning to regulate emotions effectively and assertively is a crucial step in overcoming insecurity. Through techniques such as Mindfulness meditation and assertiveness training, individuals can gain control over their emotions and react to them in a more constructive manner. This helps reduce feelings of insecurity, as individuals become more self-aware and confident in expressing their needs and desires. Regulating emotions effectively contributes to the development of healthy relationships and enhances problem-solving skills. By taking the time to understand and address their emotional experiences, individuals can overcome insecurity and lead a more fulfilling and confident life.

In today's society, insecurity is a pervasive issue that affects individuals of all ages and backgrounds. Whether it is a fear of failure, a lack of self-confidence, or a constant need for validation, insecurity can significantly hinder personal growth and overall well-being. Overcoming insecurity is not an insurmountable task; it requires introspection, self-acceptance, and a commitment to personal growth and development.

One of the first steps in overcoming insecurity is to engage in self-reflection and understand the root causes of these feelings. Insecurity is often rooted in past experiences, negative self-perception, or societal pressures. By taking the time to explore one's thoughts and emotions, individuals can begin to identify the triggers and patterns that contribute to their feelings of insecurity. This self-awareness is crucial in order to challenge and change these harmful thought patterns.

Another important aspect of overcoming insecurity is self-acceptance. Many individuals hold themselves to unrealistic standards and constantly compare themselves to others, leading to feelings of inadequacy and self-doubt. Embracing one's unique qualities and celebrating personal strengths is essential for building self-confidence and reducing insecurity. It is important to recognize that everyone has their own journey and their own set of strengths and weaknesses. By acknowledging and accepting these differences, individuals can begin to appreciate their own worth and intrinsic value. Seeking support from others can be instrumental in overcoming insecurity. Talking to trusted friends, family members, or seeking help from a mental health professional can provide valuable perspective and guidance. Individuals with insecurities isolate themselves, believing they are alone in their struggles. Reaching out to others can create a sense of connection and remind individuals that they are not alone. Support from others can also provide a safe space for individuals to share their vulnerabilities and receive encouragement and validation. Setting realistic goals and taking steps towards personal growth is crucial in overcoming insecurity. By challenging oneself and achieving small victories, individuals can gradually build confidence and overcome self-doubt. It is important to break larger goals into manageable tasks and celebrate each milestone along the way. These accomplishments act as evidence of personal growth and reinforce a positive self-image. Practicing self-care and cultivating a positive mindset are vital in overcoming insecurity. Engaging in activities that promote self-care, such as exercise, relaxation techniques, or pursuing hobbies, can help individuals reduce stress and nurture their emotional well-being. Challenging negative self-talk and reframing negative thoughts into positive affirmations can significantly impact one's self-perception. Reshaping one's mindset involves replacing self-deprecating thoughts with empowering beliefs, reinforcing self-worth and confidence. Overcoming insecurity requires individuals to embark on an introspective journey of self-reflection, self-acceptance, and personal growth. By identifying the root causes of insecurity, embracing personal strengths, seeking support, setting realistic goals, and practicing self-care, individuals can gradually overcome self-doubt and develop a strong sense of self-confidence. While the journey may be challenging, the rewards of overcoming insecurity are immense, allowing individuals to live their lives to their fullest potential.

XVII. SETTING REALISTIC EXPECTATIONS

Individuals struggling with insecurity place unrealistic standards on themselves, constantly feeling the need to meet impossibly high benchmarks. This mindset only perpetuates feelings of inadequacy and can hinder personal growth. To overcome this, individuals must learn to set realistic expectations for themselves and come to terms with their own limitations. Recognizing and accepting one's limitations does not signify weakness, but rather wisdom and self-awareness. By acknowledging what they can realistically achieve, individuals can set more attainable goals and celebrate their success, thereby fostering a positive mindset. Setting realistic expectations also involves reframing one's perspective on failure. Instead of viewing failure as evidence of personal incompetence, individuals should understand it as a steppingstone towards growth and improvement. By allowing themselves to make mistakes and learn from them, individuals can acquire new skills and develop resilience, thus combating their insecurities. Nevertheless, it is important to be mindful that setting realistic expectations does not mean settling for mediocrity. Encouraging personal growth and setting ambitious yet realistic goals is key to overcoming insecurity. Striving for continuous improvement while understanding personal limitations can lead to a sense of accomplishment and fulfillment. In setting realistic expectations, it is imperative to consider the individualistic nature of success and avoid comparing oneself to others. Each individual has their unique set of talents, strengths, and circumstances, making comparisons futile and detrimental to one's self-esteem. Rather than measuring success based on external factors or societal standards, individuals should focus on their personal growth and progress. By recognizing and acknowledging their own achievements, individuals can cultivate a sense of self-worth that is independent of others' opinions or accomplishments. Seeking validation solely from external sources can perpetuate insecurities, causing individuals to constantly seek approval and validation from others. In contrast, setting realistic expectations involves prioritizing self-acceptance and self-love, acknowledging one's inherent worth irrespective of external validation. Self-validation promotes a sense of security and confidence, alleviating feelings of insecurity and fostering a healthier self-perception. In setting realistic expectations, it is essential to consider the importance of self-care and maintaining balance in various aspects of life. Sometimes, individuals struggling with insecurity become consumed by external achievements, neglecting their physical and mental well-being. Neglecting one's self-care can lead to burnout, exacerbating feelings of inadequacy and contributing to a negative mindset. Prioritizing self-care necessitates setting realistic expectations in terms of work-life balance, leisure, and personal relationships. Allowing oneself time for relaxation, self-reflection, and pursuing hobbies outside of work can improve overall well-being and mental clarity, thus enhancing one's ability to overcome insecurity.

Setting realistic expectations is crucial for overcoming insecurity as it allows individuals to acknowledge and accept their limitations while still striving for personal growth. By reframing failure, valuing individual progress, and prioritizing self-care, individuals can develop a more positive self-perception, foster resilience, and cultivate a healthier mindset. Setting realistic expectations promotes personal growth, self-acceptance, and a sense of fulfillment, enabling individuals to overcome their insecurities and thrive.

UNDERSTANDING ONE'S LIMITATIONS AND STRENGTHS

Understanding one's limitations and strengths is crucial for personal growth and development. It requires self-reflection and a willingness to explore one's abilities and shortcomings. Recognizing limitations allows individuals to set realistic goals and make necessary adjustments to achieve them. It helps individuals focus their energies on areas where they are most competent and skilled. On the other hand, understanding strengths empowers individuals to embrace their unique qualities and utilize them to their advantage. It gives individuals the confidence to face challenges head-on, knowing that they possess the necessary skills and abilities to overcome them. Understanding one's limitations and strengths is not always a straightforward process. It requires introspection and an honest evaluation of oneself. Insecurity and self-doubt can cloud one's perception of their abilities, making it difficult to accurately assess their limitations and strengths. Overcoming this insecurity entails challenging negative self-talk and reframing one's mindset to focus on positive aspects of oneself. This can be achieved through self-affirmations and surrounding oneself with a supportive network of friends and mentors who can provide objective feedback and guidance. Seeking opportunities for personal growth and skill development can help to uncover untapped strengths and improve upon weaknesses. Engaging in new experiences and stepping outside of one's comfort zone allows for self-discovery and the development of new skills. It also fosters resilience and the ability to adapt to various situations. Embracing failure as a learning opportunity is essential when understanding one's limitations and strengths. Failure provides valuable insights into areas that may require improvement and highlights areas where strengths can be further capitalized upon. Rather than being discouraged by failure, individuals should view it as a steppingstone towards growth and self-improvement. The key is to be open to feedback, both positive and negative, and use it constructively to identify areas for personal development. Understanding one's limitations and strengths is a fundamental aspect of personal and professional growth. It requires self-reflection, an honest evaluation, and the willingness to embrace both strengths and weaknesses.

Overcoming insecurity and self-doubt is crucial in this process, as it allows individuals to accurately assess their abilities and take appropriate action to improve upon their limitations. Seeking opportunities for growth and skill development, as well as embracing failure as a learning opportunity, are vital components of understanding one's limitations and strengths. This understanding empowers individuals to set realistic goals, make necessary adjustments, and capitalize on their unique qualities. By continually striving for self-improvement and focusing on personal development, individuals can overcome their limitations, unleash their true potential, and achieve success in various aspects of life.

AVOIDING PERFECTIONISM AND UNREALISTIC STANDARDS

Perfectionism can be a problematic mindset that sets unattainable expectations and causes individuals to constantly feel like they are falling short of their goals. It is crucial to recognize that perfection is an illusionistic concept and impossibility – there will always be some room for improvement or something that could have been done differently. Acknowledging this reality can help individuals let go of their need for perfection and instead focus on progress and growth. Unrealistic standards stem from societal pressures and comparisons that can lead to decreased self-esteem and heightened insecurity. To counteract this, it is vital to define one's own standards and avoid measuring success solely by external factors. Understanding and accepting personal limitations is a significant aspect of avoiding unrealistic standards. Recognizing that mistakes are part of the learning process and that setbacks should not be seen as failures but as opportunities to grow and develop can be transformative. Shifting the focus from perfection to learning and improvement can help alleviate feelings of insecurity and foster a healthier mindset. Seeking support from friends, family, and professionals can be immensely beneficial in overcoming perfectionism and unrealistic standards. Discussing insecurities and fears with trusted individuals can provide reassurance and perspective, while professionals can offer guidance and therapeutic techniques specifically tailored to address these issues. Engaging in self-reflection and self-compassion can help challenge perfectionistic tendencies and irrational beliefs. Practicing self-awareness and reframing negative thoughts can contribute to a more positive self-perception and reduce feelings of inadequacy. Another helpful strategy to combat insecurity arising from perfectionism and unrealistic standards is setting realistic and achievable goals. Breaking down larger objectives into smaller, manageable steps can provide a sense of progress and accomplishment, which can boost self-confidence and diminish insecurity. It is important to celebrate each milestone achieved along the way, even if progress seems slow or insignificant. Embracing a growth mindset and valuing effort, resilience, and learning can also play a significant role in overcoming insecurity. Understanding that talents and skills can be developed over time through hard work and dedication can dispel the notion that one's worth is solely determined by achieving perfect outcomes. Avoiding perfectionism and unrealistic standards is a crucial aspect of overcoming insecurity. Recognizing that perfection is unattainable and that personal limitations should be embraced enables individuals to focus on growth, progress, and self-compassion. Seeking support from others, engaging in self-reflection, and setting realistic goals contribute to alleviating feelings of insecurity and fostering a healthier mindset. Embracing a growth mindset and valuing effort and resilience further reinforce the journey towards overcoming insecurity. By implementing these strategies, individuals can break free from the shackles of perfectionism and unrealistic standards, ultimately achieving a greater sense of self-acceptance and confidence.

SETTING ATTAINABLE GOALS AND CELEBRATING INCREMENTAL PROGRESS

Insecurity often stems from a fear of failure or not measuring up to others' expectations. By setting realistic and achievable goals, individuals can gradually regain their confidence and self-belief. When goals are attainable, they serve as stepping-stones towards success, making it easier to track progress and celebrate small achievements along the way. By breaking larger tasks into smaller, manageable ones, individuals can prevent themselves from feeling overwhelmed and intimidated. Celebrating incremental progress acts as positive reinforcement, motivating individuals to continue their efforts and persevere in the face of challenges. This celebration does not have to be extravagant or extravagant but can simply involve acknowledging and praising oneself for completing a task or making progress towards a goal. Even the smallest accomplishments should be recognized and appreciated as they contribute to an overall sense of achievement and self-worth. For instance, if an individual struggling with insecurity in academic performance sets a goal of improving their grades, they may start by focusing on one subject at a time. They can set a specific target, such as achieving a certain grade or understanding a particular concept. As they work towards that goal, they can break it down into smaller tasks, such as completing assignments on time or studying for a specific number of hours each day. By regularly accomplishing these tasks and achieving the desired results, they can celebrate their incremental progress. They might re-

ward themselves by treating themselves to something they enjoy or indulging in a favorite activity. This celebration not only
reinforces the positive behavior but also boosts their confidence
and motivation to tackle the next challenge. Setting realistic
goals and celebrating progress can help individuals develop a
growth mindset. Insecurity often stems from fixed beliefs, where
individuals believe their abilities and intelligence are fixed traits
that cannot be changed. By focusing on attainable goals and
recognizing progress as valuable, individuals can shift towards
a growth mindset. They come to view setbacks and failures as
opportunities for learning and growth rather than evidence of
their inadequacy. This shift in perspective allows individuals to
embrace challenges, push beyond their comfort zones, and continuously strive for improvement. By setting attainable goals
and celebrating incremental progress, individuals can foster a
sense of achievement, empowerment, and resilience while overcoming their insecurities. Overcoming insecurity requires intentional efforts, and setting attainable goals and celebrating incremental progress play essential roles in this process. By setting realistic objectives, individuals can break free from the fear
of failure or not meeting expectations. By acknowledging and
celebrating even the smallest achievements along the way, individuals can boost their confidence, reinforce positive behavior,
and develop a growth mindset. Through this combination of
goal setting and celebrating progress, individuals can build a
solid foundation of self-belief, resilience, and personal growth,
ultimately leaving their feelings of insecurity behind.

It is crucial to recognize that overcoming insecurity is an ongoing process that requires dedication and self-reflection. This
paragraph will discuss the importance of developing a positive

self-image, fostering healthy relationships, and seeking professional help to combat the deep-rooted nature of insecurities. One of the initial steps to overcoming insecurity is cultivating a positive self-image. This involves challenging negative self-talk and embracing self-acceptance. Individuals should consciously monitor their internal dialogue and challenge negative thoughts by replacing them with positive affirmations. By acknowledging one's strengths and accomplishments, one can gradually build a healthier self-image. Embracing personal imperfections and understanding that everyone possesses flaws can reduce the constant self-criticism that fuels insecurity. Fostering healthy relationships plays a crucial role in overcoming insecurity. Surrounding oneself with supportive individuals who genuinely care about one's well-being can enhance self-esteem. Close friends and family members can provide validation and encouragement, reinforcing a positive self-image. Engaging in meaningful and fulfilling relationships helps combat feelings of loneliness and inadequacy. By developing strong connections with others, individuals can experience a sense of belonging and acceptance, which can counteract the negative narratives associated with insecurity. Seeking professional help is another essential aspect of overcoming insecurity. In many cases, insecurities are deeply rooted and may require professional intervention to be fully addressed. Therapists and counselors can provide guidance and support in overcoming insecurities, offering various therapeutic techniques and coping strategies tailored to individual needs. Through therapy, individuals can reconnect with their emotions, identify the underlying causes of their insecurities, and develop healthier thought patterns. Therapy can assist in challenging irrational beliefs, such as constant comparison to others or needing validation from external sources. Therapists can help individuals develop practical skills to improve self-confidence and assertiveness, ultimately leading to a more fulfilling and confident life. Overcoming insecurity requires a multifaceted approach that involves developing a positive self-image, fostering healthy relationships, and seeking professional help when necessary. The journey towards self-acceptance and confidence is a continuous process, demanding self-reflection, perseverance, and external support. By challenging negative self-talk, embracing personal imperfections, and acknowledging strengths, individuals can gradually build a healthier self-image. Surrounding oneself with supportive individuals who genuinely care can enhance self-esteem and counteract the negative narratives associated with insecurity. Professional intervention through therapy is crucial in addressing deeply rooted insecurities. Therapists can guide individuals in reconnecting with their emotions, identifying the underlying causes of their insecurities, and implementing practical coping strategies. By incorporating these strategies into one's life, individuals can pave the way towards self-acceptance, a positive mindset, and a more fulfilling and confident future.

XVIII. INVESTING IN PERSONAL DEVELOPMENT

One must continuously work on oneself to build self-confidence and resilience. There are various ways to invest in personal development, and each individual must find what works best for them. One effective approach is setting personal goals and creating a plan to achieve them. By setting achievable goals, individuals can experience a sense of accomplishment, which boosts self-esteem and reduces feelings of insecurity. Pursuing hobbies and interests outside of one's comfort zone can significantly contribute to personal growth. Exploring new activities not only expands one's skill set but also enhances self-confidence by pushing one's boundaries and proving to themselves that they are capable of learning and developing new talents. Seeking opportunities for learning and self-improvement is crucial for personal development. Attending seminars, workshops, or enrolling in online courses can provide new knowledge, skills, and perspectives, helping individuals develop a more comprehensive understanding of themselves and the world around them. Investing in personal development involves taking care of one's physical and mental well-being. Engaging in regular exercise, getting enough sleep, and maintaining a balanced diet are all essential for overall health. Prioritizing self-care not only boosts confidence but also equips individuals with the energy and mental clarity necessary to face challenges and overcome insecurities. Investing in personal development includes developing strong and meaningful relationships. Surrounding oneself with supportive and positive individuals can greatly contribute to personal growth. Engaging in deep conversations, seeking advice, and receiving constructive feedback from trusted friends or mentors can provide valuable insights, foster new perspectives, and offer emotional support during moments of insecurity. Investing in personal development requires individuals to confront their fears and embrace vulnerability. Stepping out of one's comfort zone and taking risks may feel intimidating, but it is in these moments of discomfort where personal growth occurs. By embracing vulnerability, individuals can learn to overcome fears, build resilience, and develop a stronger sense of self. Investing in personal development is an essential aspect of overcoming insecurity.

By setting goals, pursuing new hobbies, seeking opportunities for learning, taking care of physical and mental well-being, developing meaningful relationships, and embracing vulnerability, individuals can actively work on building self-confidence and resilience. Overcoming insecurity is a gradual and ongoing process, and investing in personal growth is a pathway towards personal fulfillment and a more secure and confident self.

PURSUING KNOWLEDGE AND SKILLS TO ENHANCE SELF-CONFIDENCE

When individuals actively seek out new information and develop their skills, they become more knowledgeable and competent in various aspects of life. This increased knowledge and competence directly contribute to a boost in self-confidence. By constantly expanding their understanding and capabilities, individuals develop a sense of mastery over their areas of interest, which in turn leads to increased self-assurance. For example, someone who takes the initiative to learn about public speaking and practice speaking in front of others will gradually become more confident in their ability to effectively communicate their ideas. Acquiring knowledge and skills empowers individuals to overcome challenges and face new situations with confidence. As they gather knowledge, individuals become equipped with the tools and strategies necessary to resolve problems and navigate unfamiliar circumstances. This ability to adapt and problem-solve instills a sense of confidence in one's abilities. For instance, someone who has gained expertise in financial management will feel more secure and confident in making investment decisions, as they have acquired the necessary knowledge to analyze risks and anticipate returns. By pursuing knowledge and skills, individuals are continuously improving themselves, which naturally boosts self-esteem. As they acquire new knowledge and develop their skills, they witness their own progression and growth. This serves as a powerful motivator and builds a positive self-perception, bolstering self-confidence. For example, someone who dedicates time and effort to learning a new language will experience a sense of accomplishment as they become more proficient, resulting in increased self-assurance in their abilities. Pursuing knowledge and skills allows individuals to discover and develop their passions and interests. When individuals engage in activities and subjects they are passionate about, they become more invested and dedicated, leading to a stronger sense of self-confidence. For instance, someone who pursues their passion for painting and actively develops their artistic skills will feel a heightened sense of self-worth and confidence as they witness the beauty they can create. Pursuing knowledge and skills is imperative for enhancing self-confidence. It enables individuals to expand their knowledge, develop abilities, and gain a sense of mastery in different areas. By continually challenging themselves and acquiring new capabilities, individuals become better equipped to overcome challenges and navigate unfamiliar situations, which generates a sense of confidence. The process of pursuing knowledge and skills inherently leads to personal growth and improvement, reinforcing positive self-perception and self-esteem. Engaging in activities and subjects individuals are passionate about encourages a deeper investment and dedication to their own development, fostering higher levels of self-confidence. The pursuit of knowledge and skills is a transformative journey that enables individuals to overcome insecurities and embrace their full potential.

SEEKING OPPORTUNITIES FOR GROWTH AND LEARNING

In order to build self-esteem and strengthen one's core identity, it is essential to continuously seek new experiences and knowledge. By actively engaging in activities that challenge our capabilities and push us outside of our comfort zones, we not only expand our horizons but also develop valuable skills and a sense of personal accomplishment. This process of seeking growth and learning is a journey that requires patience, resilience, and open-mindedness. It begins with a genuine desire to improve oneself and a willingness to embrace the unknown.

One way to seek opportunities for growth and learning is through education. College, for example, provides a valuable platform for intellectual exploration and personal development. Students are exposed to a diverse range of subjects and teachings, allowing them to broaden their perspectives and refine their critical thinking skills. Engaging in academic discourse and research stimulates intellectual curiosity and encourages the pursuit of new knowledge. Likewise, being part of a college community offers countless opportunities for personal growth, such as joining clubs, participating in extracurricular activities, or taking on leadership roles. The college experience is a transformative time in which individuals can discover their passions, explore new interests, and cultivate lifelong learning habits.

Beyond the confines of academia, seeking opportunities for growth and learning can manifest in various aspects of life. Professional development, for instance, is a key area where one can continually grow and learn. Taking advantage of trainings, workshops, and conferences can enhance skills, expand knowledge, and boost confidence in the workplace. Seeking mentorship or guidance from more experienced individuals in one's field can provide valuable insights and help navigate the challenges of professional growth. Embracing new challenges and embracing a growth mindset can lead to increased job satisfaction and improved career prospects.

Personal relationships also offer opportunities for growth and learning. Engaging in meaningful con versations, actively listening to others, and seeking constructive feedback can greatly contribute to personal growth and improved relationships. By building emotional intelligence and being open to different perspectives, individuals develop better communication skills and gain a deeper understanding of themselves and others. Seeking new friendships and connecting with diverse groups of people can broaden one's worldview, challenge preconceived notions, and foster personal growth through exposure to different beliefs and experiences. Seeking opportunities for growth and learning requires individuals to step outside of their comfort zones and embrace change. It is a continuous process that demands a certain level of vulnerability and willingness to take risks.

By exploring new avenues of knowledge, engaging in personal and professional development, and cultivating meaningful relationships, individuals can strive towards their full potential and overcome insecurities. The journey towards growth and learning is not always easy, but the rewards in terms of personal fulfillment, confidence, and self-esteem are immeasurable.

Embracing a mindset of growth and actively pursuing opportunities for growth and learning is the key to overcoming insecurities and unlocking one's true potential in life.

ENGAGING IN CONTINUOUS SELF-IMPROVEMENT

Insecurity often stems from a lack of confidence in oneself and one's abilities, and self-improvement is a powerful tool to combat these feelings. Engaging in continuous self-improvement allows individuals to develop new skills, enhance their knowledge, and broaden their perspective. By actively seeking personal growth and development, individuals can build their self-esteem and gain a sense of accomplishment.

One way to engage in continuous self-improvement is through education. College, in particular, provides an ideal platform for individuals to expand their knowledge and acquire new skills. Taking advantage of the vast array of courses and resources available on campus can help individuals gain a deeper understanding of their fields of interest and boost their confidence. Actively participating in class discussions, engaging with professors, and seeking out additional learning opportunities can further enhance one's educational experience and promote personal growth. Engaging in continuous self-improvement also involves seeking out challenges and stepping out of one's comfort zone. When individuals challenge themselves, they push their limits and discover new capabilities they may not have known existed. By taking on new challenges and overcoming them, individuals gain confidence in their abilities to navigate unfamiliar situations. For example, joining clubs or organizations on campus, participating in leadership roles, or even pursuing internships or research projects allows individuals to cultivate important skills such as teamwork, problem-solving, and communication. These experiences not only contribute to personal growth but also serve as concrete evidence of one's abilities, helping combat feelings of insecurity.

Another aspect of continuous self-improvement is embracing failure as an opportunity for learning and growth. Insecurity often stems from fear of failure and criticism. By reframing failure as an essential part of the learning process, individuals can overcome these insecurities and approach challenges with a growth mindset. Embracing failure as an opportunity for learning means actively seeking feedback, reflecting on one's mistakes, and making necessary adjustments. It also involves being resilient and persevering in the face of setbacks, ultimately leading to personal growth and increased self-confidence.

Engaging in continuous self-improvement includes self-reflection and setting realistic goals. By regularly evaluating one's strengths and weaknesses, individuals can identify areas for improvement and work towards specific objectives. Setting achievable goals allows individuals to measure their progress and experience a sense of accomplishment, boosting their self-esteem. Seeking feedback from mentors, peers, or trusted individuals can provide valuable insights and guidance to further enhance personal growth. Engaging in continuous self-improvement is crucial for overcoming insecurity. By actively seeking personal growth through education, challenging oneself, embracing failure, and setting realistic goals, individuals can build confidence and combat feelings of insecurity. Through these processes, individuals enhance their skills, broaden their perspective, and gain a sense of accomplishment, ultimately leading to a greater sense of self-assurance.

In today's society, insecurity has become a prevalent issue that affects individuals across all age groups. While it is a natural human emotion to some extent, allowing insecurity to consume one's life can have detrimental effects. There are various steps that individuals can take to overcome this insecurity and lead a more fulfilling life. Firstly, it is crucial to acknowledge and identify the underlying causes of one's insecurity. This could be a result of various factors such as past traumas, negative self-perception, or societal pressures. By understanding the root causes, individuals can gain insight into themselves and develop strategies to overcome their insecurities. Seeking therapy or counseling can be particularly helpful in this aspect, as it provides individuals with a safe space to explore their feelings and emotions, and allows them to work through their insecurities with the guidance of a professional. Secondly, it is important to practice self-compassion and self-care. Individuals who struggle with insecurity are overly critical of themselves and engage in negative self-talk. By practicing self-compassion, individuals can develop a kinder and more understanding attitude towards themselves. This involves treating oneself with the same kindness and empathy that they would offer to a friend going through a difficult time. Engaging in self-care activities that promote emotional and physical well-being can also aid in overcoming insecurity. This could include activities such as exercising, practicing Mindfulness, journaling, or engaging in hobbies that bring joy and relaxation. Thirdly, challenging negative thoughts and beliefs is a crucial step in overcoming insecurity. Insecurities often stem from negative self-perception and distorted thinking patterns. By actively challenging these negative thoughts and replacing them with more positive and realistic ones, individuals can gradually shift their mindset and improve their self-esteem. This can be done through various techniques such as cognitive-behavioral therapy, affirmations, or keeping a gratitude journal. Surrounding oneself with a supportive network of friends and family can also play a significant role in overcoming insecurity. Having a strong support system provides individuals with encouragement, validation, and reassurance, which can help to counteract feelings of insecurity. It is important to communicate with loved ones about one's insecurities and allow them to offer support and understanding. Interacting with individuals who have similar experiences can also be beneficial, as it allows individuals to see that they are not alone in their struggles. It is crucial to set realistic goals and celebrate small victories. Individuals with insecurity may fear failure and hold themselves back from achieving their full potential. By setting realistic goals and taking small steps towards success, individuals can gradually build their confidence and overcome their insecurities. Celebrating even the smallest victories along the way can help to reinforce a positive self-image and provide motivation to continue on the path of growth and self-improvement. Overcoming insecurity is a lifelong journey that requires self-reflection, self-compassion, and determination. By acknowledging and understanding the causes of one's insecurity, practicing self-care, challenging negative thoughts, seeking a support system, and setting realistic goals, individuals can break free from the chains of insecurity and lead a more confident and fulfilling life.

XIX. SURROUNDING ONESELF WITH POSITIVE INFLUENCES

In the journey towards overcoming insecurity, it is crucial to surround oneself with positive influences. The environment and people around us play a significant role in shaping our thoughts, beliefs, and overall outlook on life. By consciously choosing to surround ourselves with individuals who exude positivity, we can create a support system that encourages personal growth and resilience. Positive influences can come in various forms from family and friends to mentors and role models. These individuals possess qualities that inspire and uplift us, making us believe in our own capabilities and potential. Being in the company of positive thinkers allows us to see beyond our insecurities and helps us in cultivating a more positive self-image.

Family, as the primary influence in our lives, can have a profound impact on our sense of self-worth. When surrounded by a family that is supportive, nurturing, and loving, we are more likely to develop a strong foundation of self-confidence. Family members who offer reassurance, celebrate our achievements, and provide a safe space for vulnerability can counteract any insecurities that may arise. Their belief in us becomes our belief in ourselves, giving us the strength to overcome feelings of inadequacy. Friends can serve as influential figures in boosting our self-esteem and promoting a positive mindset. We tend to adopt the attitudes and behaviors of those we spend the most time with, and thus, it is vital to choose friends who uplift and empower us. Positive friends not only offer encouragement but also challenge us to push our limits and reach our fullest potential. Sharing goals, dreams, and aspirations with like-minded individuals can foster a sense of belonging and make us realize that we are not alone in our insecurities. Having mentors and role models can be immensely beneficial in overcoming insecurity. Mentors are individuals who have successfully navigated similar challenges and can provide guidance and wisdom throughout our personal growth journey. Being mentored by someone who has overcome their own insecurities can instill confidence in our ability to do the same. Role models, on the other hand, are individuals we admire and look up to, often because they have achieved great things. Observing their achievements and learning about their journey can inspire us to develop a positive mindset and belief in our own potential.

Supplementing these personal relationships, surrounding oneself with positive influences also includes external factors such as media consumption and the environment in which one engages. By choosing to expose oneself to uplifting and inspiring content, such as motivational books, podcasts, and movies, individuals can reinforce positive thinking and expand their mindset. Similarly, engaging in activities and joining communities that align with one's values and interests can also provide a positive and supportive environment. Surrounding oneself with positive influences is crucial in overcoming insecurity. Whether it is the unwavering support of family, the empowering influence of friends, the guidance of mentors, or the inspiration from role models these positive influences shape our self-perception and help us develop a resilient and confident mindset.

By creating a network of positivity, individuals can transcend their insecurities and embrace a more positive self-image,

thereby fostering personal growth and achieving their fullest
potential.

EVALUATING THE IMPACT OF SOCIAL CIRCLE ON SELF-ESTEEM

Another crucial factor to consider in overcoming insecurity is evaluating the impact of one's social circle on their self-esteem. Humans are inherently social beings, and the relationships we form with others can significantly influence our self-perception, confidence, and overall well-being. It is no surprise, then, that the quality of our relationships and the people we surround ourselves with can either boost or hinder our self-esteem. Firstly, a positive and supportive social circle can contribute to a healthier sense of self-worth. When individuals have friends or acquaintances who appreciate them, offer encouragement, and provide validation, they are more likely to develop a positive self-image. These relationships create an environment where individuals feel accepted, valued, and appreciated, enabling them to feel more confident and secure in themselves. On the other hand, negative or toxic relationships can have detrimental effects on self-esteem. When surrounded by critical, judgmental, or emotionally abusive individuals, individuals can internalize these negative messages and start to believe them. Continuous exposure to such negativity erodes an individual's self-worth, leading to insecurities and feelings of inadequacy. Not only does this impact their self-esteem, but it also affects their overall mental health. The impact of one's social circle on self-esteem can also extend to societal norms and expectations. Societies often have specific beauty standards, societal norms, and unattainable ideals that dictate what is considered attractive, successful, or worthy. These ideals are perpetuated and reinforced through various sources, including media, advertising, and social interactions. When individuals do not align with these narrow standards, they can suffer from low self-esteem and feelings of insecurity. For instance, body image concerns are prevalent, with individuals feeling pressured to maintain a perfect physique, which can lead to a negative body image and self-worth. In such cases, the social circle can either support or break these societal norms, significantly affecting one's self-esteem. Supportive friends who value diversity, inclusivity, and empathy can challenge these societal norms and cultivate a more positive self-image by embracing individuality and uniqueness. Conversely, judgmental or conforming social circles can reinforce the negative impact of societal norms, perpetuating insecurities and lowering self-esteem.

Evaluating the impact of one's social circle on self-esteem plays a vital role in overcoming insecurities. Positive and supportive relationships can significantly contribute to a healthier self-perception, fostering confidence and security within individuals. Conversely, negative or toxic relationships can erode self-worth and lead to feelings of inadequacy. Societal norms and expectations perpetuated by one's social circle can also impact self-esteem, as individuals may feel pressured to fit into narrow standards of beauty or success. It is crucial for individuals to surround themselves with supportive and accepting friends who challenge societal norms and embrace uniqueness. By doing so, individuals can cultivate a stronger sense of self and overcome their insecurities, leading to overall improved well-being.

BUILDING RELATIONSHIPS WITH INDIVIDUALS WHO UPLIFT AND SUPPORT

Insecurities often stem from negative past experiences or self-doubt, and having a strong support system can provide the boost of confidence needed to overcome these feelings. Surrounding oneself with positive and encouraging people creates an environment of acceptance and love that can help negate the negative thoughts and beliefs that fuel insecurities. When individuals uplift and support one another, they provide a safe space where vulnerabilities can be shared and validated, resulting in personal growth and increased self-esteem. Building relationships with those who uplift and support also offers opportunities for learning and personal development. As humans, we constantly learn from our interactions and experiences, and being surrounded by positive influences enables us to acquire new coping mechanisms and perspectives that can further aid in overcoming insecurities. These relationships offer a support system that understands and acknowledges our struggles, providing encouragement and guidance when we need it the most. In addition, individuals who uplift and support can also serve as role models and inspire us to aspire towards greater self-confidence and personal growth. By observing their own journeys of resilience and self-acceptance, we can learn valuable lessons that can be applied to our own lives.

Building relationships with uplifting and supportive individuals also promotes a sense of belonging and community. Insecurities often make individuals feel isolated and disconnected from others, amplifying their negative thoughts and limiting their potential for growth. When individuals forge connections with those who uplift and support, they no longer feel alone in their struggles. This sense of belonging cultivates a shared understanding of one another's experiences and fosters an environment where individuals can celebrate one another's successes. In this supportive community, everyone is encouraged to embrace their vulnerabilities, as they know they will be met with empathy and love. These relationships provide individuals with the opportunity to connect with others who have gone through similar experiences, enabling them to feel validated and understood.

Building relationships with uplifting and supportive individuals can also offer opportunities for collaboration and personal empowerment. These individuals can serve as mentors or allies, guiding us towards self-improvement and helping us develop skills and talents that we aspire to cultivate. Their support and belief in our abilities can instill a sense of confidence and motivation, leading to personal empowerment and a stronger sense of self. Collaborating with them on projects and goals can also foster a sense of achievement and purpose, allowing us to showcase our strengths and contribute to a meaningful cause. In this way, building relationships with individuals who uplift and support can not only help us overcome insecurities but also enable us to thrive and reach our full potential.

LIMITING EXPOSURE TO NEGATIVE INFLUENCES OR TOXIC RELATIONSHIPS

Insecurities can often be fueled or exacerbated by the constant negative feedback or toxic behaviors of those around us. Whether it is a friend, a family member, or even a romantic partner, engaging with individuals who consistently bring us down or undermine our self-esteem can be detrimental to our mental health and overall confidence. It is essential to recognize and acknowledge these toxic relationships and take necessary steps to limit our exposure to them. This may involve setting clear boundaries, distancing ourselves, or even cutting ties with these individuals altogether. Although it can be challenging or even daunting to sever connections with people we once considered important in our lives, it is crucial for our personal growth and well-being. Surrounding ourselves with positive and supportive people who uplift us and encourage our strengths can contribute significantly to building our self-esteem and reducing our insecurities. By consciously choosing our relationships and engaging with individuals who value and respect us, we are more likely to develop a healthier self-image and a stronger sense of self-worth. Limiting exposure to negative influences extends beyond toxic relationships and encompass es various external factors that can impact our insecurities. As individuals living in the digital age, we are constantly bombarded with unrealistic beauty standards, idealized lifestyles, and the achievements of others, which can easily trigger feelings of inadequacy or insecurity. Social media platforms, in particular, have become breeding grounds for comparison and self-doubt. Spending hours scrolling through perfectly curated feeds and comparing ourselves to others' highlight reels can lead to a distorted perception of reality and contribute to our insecurities. It is essential to be mindful of our digital consumption and take regular breaks from social media to protect our mental well-being. Instead, focusing on activities that bring us joy, engaging in hobbies, or building genuine connections with others can help redirect our attention away from such negative influences and foster a sense of positivity and self-acceptance.

Overcoming insecurity entails limiting exposure to negative influences or toxic relationships. By actively recognizing and addressing toxic individuals in our lives and making conscious efforts to distance ourselves from them, we can protect our mental well-being and cultivate healthier and more fulfilling relationships. Being mindful of the negative influences we encounter externally, such as unrealistic beauty standards perpetuated by social media, is crucial for maintaining a positive self-image. By prioritizing activities and connections that uplift us and foster positivity, we can gradually build our self-esteem, reduce our insecurities, and embark on a journey of personal growth and self-acceptance. While it may require bold choices and moments of discomfort, the rewards of limiting exposure to negativity and fostering healthier relationships far outweigh the temporary discomfort, as we pave the way for a more fulfilling and secure sense of self.A crucial step in overcoming insecurity is to challenge negative thoughts and beliefs. Insecurities are often fueled by self-critical thoughts and beliefs that undermine one's self-worth. It is imperative to identify and examine these negative thoughts, questioning their validity and replacing them with more positive and realistic ones. For instance, if someone believes they are not intelligent enough to succeed academically, they may need to challenge this belief by acknowledging their past achievements or seeking evidence of their abilities. Practicing self-compassion and reframing negative self-talk can greatly aid in challenging insecurities. Rather than berating oneself for past failures, it is essential to offer understanding and kindness towards oneself, just as one would towards a close friend. Cultivating self-compassion helps to break the cycle of self-judgment and allows individuals to view themselves in a more balanced and accepting light.

Seeking support from others can be incredibly beneficial in overcoming insecurity. Opening up and sharing one's insecurities with trusted friends or family members can foster a sense of validation and understanding. Individuals discover that they are not alone in their struggles, which can provide a sense of relief and reassurance. Seeking professional help, such as therapy or counseling, can provide individuals with the tools and guidance needed to conquer their insecurities. Therapists are trained to help individuals explore the root causes of their insecurities and develop coping strategies to manage them effectively. Through therapy, individuals can gain valuable insights into their insecurities and learn new skills to build their self-esteem and confidence. Insecurity is a common and deeply rooted issue that can hinder individuals from reaching their full potential and enjoying fulfilling relationships. By understanding the underlying causes of insecurity and implementing specific strategies, individuals can work towards overcoming their insecurities. First and foremost, identifying the triggers and acknowledging the impact of past experiences is paramount.

Building self-esteem through self-care and cultivating a positive self-image can also aid in overcoming insecurity. Challenging negative thoughts and seeking support from others are crucial steps in the journey towards self-acceptance and confidence. Overcoming insecurity is not an overnight process, but with commitment and self-compassion, individuals can gradually break free from the shackles of their insecurities and embrace a more empowered and fulfilling life.

XX. PRACTICING GRATITUDE

Practicing gratitude is a powerful tool for overcoming insecurity. In a society that constantly bombards individuals with messages of what they should have or who they should be, it can be easy to fall into a mindset of scarcity or inadequacy. By cultivating a practice of gratitude, individuals can shift their focus from what they lack to what they already possess, leading to a more secure and contented mindset. Gratitude allows individuals to recognize and appreciate the abundance in their lives, whether it be in the form of supportive relationships, material possessions, or personal achievements. By acknowledging and expressing gratitude for these blessings, individuals can counteract the feelings of insecurity that stem from a sense of lack.

One way to practice gratitude is through the deliberate act of reflecting on the positive aspects of life. This can be done through journaling, meditation, or simply taking a few moments each day to mentally list three things for which one is grateful. Engaging in this practice encourages individuals to redirect their attention towards the good things they already have, rather than dwelling on perceived inadequacies. Research has shown that this simple act of gratitude can have profound effects on mental well-being and overall life satisfaction. In a study conducted by Emmons and McCullough (2003), participants who engaged in a daily gratitude journaling exercise experienced greater levels of positive affect, optimism, and overall life satisfaction compared to those who did not engage in such practice. By consistently acknowledging and appreciating the positive aspects of life, individuals can build a foundation of security and contentment. Another way to practice gratitude is by expressing it towards others. Taking the time to express appreciation for others' kindness, support, or companionship not only strengthens relationships but also fosters a sense of security within oneself. By acknowledging the positive impact others have on our lives, we reinforce the belief that we are worthy of love, care, and support. This can be done through simple acts of kindness, such as writing a thank-you note, sending a heartfelt message, or verbally expressing gratitude. Research has shown that expressing gratitude towards others can lead to increased prosocial behavior, improved relationships, and enhanced well-being (Algoe et al., 2010). By actively practicing gratitude towards others, individuals can create a positive feedback loop that bolsters their own feelings of security.

Practicing gratitude is a transformative practice that can help individuals overcome insecurity by shifting their mindset from scarcity to abundance. By intentionally focusing on the positive aspects of life and expressing gratitude towards others, individuals cultivate a sense of security and contentment within themselves. This practice allows them to recognize their own worth and value, embracing the blessings they already possess rather than perpetually striving for more. Through gratitude, individuals can break free from the shackles of insecurity and embrace a more fulfilled and secure existence.

RECOGNIZING AND APPRECIATING ONE'S BLESSINGS AND ACCOMPLISHMENTS

All too often, individuals become so consumed by their fears and insecurities that they fail to recognize the positive aspects of their lives. By taking the time to reflect on and appreciate their blessings and accomplishments, individuals can gain a newfound sense of confidence and self-worth. A crucial aspect of recognizing blessings and accomplishments is practicing gratitude. Gratitude allows individuals to shift their focus from what they lack to what they have, enabling them to appreciate the abundance in their lives. Research has shown that practicing gratitude can lead to increased happiness and life satisfaction. Individuals who are grateful are more likely to have lower levels of stress and depression. By cultivating a gratitude practice, individuals can train their minds to recognize and appreciate the positive aspects of their lives, which in turn can help counter feelings of insecurity. Reflecting on past accomplishments can be an effective way to gain a sense of pride and self-assurance. Individuals with insecurities tend to downplay their achievements and dismiss their successes as mere luck or coincidence. By acknowledging and celebrating their accomplishments, individuals can build a more positive self-perception. Reflecting on past successes can provide individuals with evidence of their capabilities and strengths, reinforcing their belief in their own abilities. This can prove particularly important in challenging times when doubts and insecurities may resurface. In addition, seeking validation from others can play a crucial role in recognizing one's blessings and accomplishments. While it is important not to solely rely on external validation, receiving recognition from others can serve as a powerful reminder of one's worth. Whether it be through positive feedback, awards, or simply acknowledging compliments, external validation can help individuals see themselves through the eyes of others and gain a more realistic perspective on their abilities and achievements. It is important not to become overly dependent on external validation, as this can undermine one's self-esteem in the long run. Recognizing and appreciating one's blessings and accomplishments goes beyond a mere act of self-validation. It is a vital step towards building resilience, combatting insecurities, and fostering a more positive and confident self-perception. By practicing gratitude, reflecting on past accomplishments, and seeking validation from others, individuals can develop a greater sense of self-worth and overcome the grip of insecurity. With this newfound appreciation for their blessings and accomplishments, individuals can embark on a journey towards self-acceptance and personal growth, ultimately leading to a more fulfilling and secure life.

SHIFTING FOCUS TOWARDS GRATITUDE RATHER THAN DWELLING ON INSECURITIES

In a society where comparison is omnipresent and insecurities are rampant, it is essential to shift our focus towards gratitude instead of dwelling on our insecurities. The constant exposure to social media and the pressure to conform to unrealistic beauty standards have fueled the rise in insecurity among individuals. By changing our perspective and adopting an attitude of gratitude, we can begin to combat these insecurities. Gratitude allows us to channel our attention towards the positive aspects of our lives and appreciate what we already have. It encourages us to acknowledge the blessings and opportunities that come our way, rather than fixating on our perceived flaws and shortcomings. By practicing gratitude, we can enhance our self-esteem and develop a healthier self-image. Instead of constantly comparing ourselves to others and belittling our own achievements, gratitude prompts us to celebrate our accomplishments and recognize our worth. This shift in mindset ultimately leads to an improved sense of self-worth and a reduction in insecurity. Focusing on gratitude allows us to cultivate a more positive and optimistic outlook on life. When we are grateful for the things we have, we become more aware of the abundance around us. We start to notice the simple pleasures and small victories in our everyday lives. This heightened awareness brings about a greater sense of fulfillment and contentment, diminishing the need to constantly seek validation from external sources. Rather than dwelling on our insecurities and fixating on what we lack, gratitude encourages us to appreciate the present moment and find joy in the little things. This shift in focus can have a profound impact on our overall mental well-being and help us overcome our insecurities.

Gratitude fosters a sense of interconnectedness and encourages the practice of empathy and compassion. By focusing on what we are grateful for, we begin to recognize the efforts and contributions of others in our lives. This newfound sense of appreciation allows us to cultivate stronger relationships and deepen our connections with others. As we become more aware of the support and love that surrounds us, we are reminded that we are not alone in our struggles. This realization can provide solace and comfort when faced with feelings of insecurity. Expressing gratitude towards others helps to alleviate our own insecurities by shifting the focus away from ourselves. When we demonstrate kindness and gratitude towards others, we contribute to a more positive and uplifting environment, creating a ripple effect that can inspire others to do the same.

Shifting our focus towards gratitude rather than dwelling on insecurities is a powerful tool for overcoming our self-doubt and negativity. By embracing gratitude, we can enhance our self-esteem, develop a positive outlook on life, and foster stronger connections with others. It is through gratitude that we can break free from the cycle of comparison and cultivate a deeper sense of self-acceptance. It is crucial for individuals to actively practice gratitude and incorporate it into their daily lives in order to overcome insecurity and lead a happier, more fulfilling life.

ENGAGING IN GRATITUDE EXERCISES SUCH AS JOURNALING OR VERBAL EXPRESSIONS

Insecurity often stems from a scarcity mindset, where individuals constantly feel that they lack or are inadequate in some way. Practicing gratitude can help shift this mindset by focusing on what one does have rather than what one lacks. Journaling is one form of gratitude exercise that involves writing down things one is grateful for on a daily basis. This practice allows individuals to reflect on the positive aspects of their life and redirect their attention away from their insecurities. By acknowledging and documenting these moments of gratitude, individuals can begin to recognize the abundance in their lives and thereby combat feelings of insecurity. Verbal expressions of gratitude, whether through conversations or affirmations, can also be powerful tools in building self-confidence and reducing insecurities. For instance, sharing appreciation with friends, family, or colleagues for their support or kindness can strengthen relationships and create a sense of connection and appreciation. Affirmations, or positive statements about oneself, can help rewire negative thought patterns often associated with insecurity. By regularly expressing gratitude for one's strengths, accomplishments, and unique qualities, individuals can slowly shift their focus towards self-acceptance and begin to recognize their own worth. Engaging in gratitude exercises can also foster a sense of perspective. Insecurity is often accompanied by a hyper-focus on one's own flaws and perceived inadequacies. By actively practicing gratitude, individuals can gain a broader perspective and realize that everyone faces challenges and has their own insecurities. This newfound perspective can not only alleviate feelings of isolation and self-doubt but also encourage empathy and understanding towards others. Gratitude exercises can also be a powerful tool for personal growth and self-reflection. By regularly engaging in these exercises, individuals can develop a greater awareness of their values, goals, and aspirations. This self-reflection enables individuals to recognize their own progress and accomplishments, leading to increased self-esteem and decreased insecurity. Gratitude exercises can help individuals identify areas for improvement and set realistic goals for personal development. By acknowledging and expressing gratitude for where one currently stands, individuals gain the confidence to move forward and strive for personal growth. Gratitude exercises provide an opportunity to practice Mindfulness. Insecurity often stems from rumination on past failures or anxieties about the future. Gratitude exercises encourage individuals to be present and fully engaged in the present moment. Whether through mindful journaling or verbal expressions of gratitude, individuals are compelled to pay attention to the positive aspects of their current experience. This practice of Mindfulness not only improves mental well-being but also generates a sense of peace and contentment, reducing the power of insecurity in one's life. Engaging in gratitude exercises such as journaling or verbal expressions is a valuable strategy for overcoming insecurity. By shifting one's focus towards gratitude, individuals can challenge their scarcity mindset, foster perspective and personal growth, practice Mindfulness, and ultimately build self-confidence. Through these practices, individuals can begin to confront and overcome their insecurities, leading to a greater sense of self-acceptance and overall well-being.

Insecurity is a prevalent issue that affects individuals across different stages of life. At the college-level, many students grapple with insecurities that hinder their academic performance, social interactions, and personal growth. Overcoming insecurity, however, is an essential step towards achieving success and fulfillment. One effective strategy to conquer insecurity in college is by focusing on self-acceptance and embracing one's unique qualities and strengths. To begin with, college students must develop a sense of self-acceptance. Insecurity often stems from a lack of confidence in oneself and a constant comparison to others. By accepting one's flaws and imperfections, students can empower themselves to rise above insecurities and build their self-esteem. Embracing imperfections and understanding that they are an integral part of individuality fosters self-love and appreciation. By acknowledging that everyone has strengths and weaknesses, students can develop a more positive mindset, free from the burden of self-doubt.

Embracing one's unique qualities and strengths is crucial in overcoming insecurity. In college, students often feel the pressure to conform to societal standards and expectations, causing them to question their worth and abilities. By identifying and celebrating their inherent talents and skills, students can replace self-doubt with self-assurance. Engaging in activities that showcase their strengths and passions not only boosts their confidence but also helps them develop a sense of purpose and direction. For instance, a student who excels in writing can join a campus literary club, participate in writing competitions, or seek internships in publishing houses. By focusing on their strengths, students can gain a sense of competence and reaffirm their self-worth. In addition to these strategies, seeking support from peers, mentors, and college resources is essential in overcoming insecurity. College campuses offer numerous resources, such as counseling centers and support groups, that cater to the well-being and personal growth of students. Sharing concerns and fears with trusted individuals can provide a fresh perspective and validate emotions, reducing the isolation and shame associated with insecurity. Peers who have experienced similar struggles can offer empathy and advice, while mentors can provide guidance and encouragement. Taking advantage of campus clubs and organizations can foster a sense of belonging and create a support network that helps alleviate insecurities. Adopting a growth mindset is crucial for overcoming insecurity. Students must understand that personal growth and learning are ongoing processes. Embracing challenges and failures as opportunities for growth rather than sources of insecurity promotes resilience and perseverance. By reframing setbacks as valuable learning experiences, students reduce the fear of failure and develop a positive outlook on their abilities. Adopting a growth mindset encourages students to view each obstacle as a steppingstone towards personal and academic development. Insecurity is a common challenge faced by college students that can hinder their academic and personal success. By focusing on self-acceptance, embracing one's unique qualities and strengths, seeking support, and adopting a growth mindset, students can overcome insecurity and develop a sense of confidence and self-assurance.

Overcoming insecurity is not an overnight process but requires consistent effort and self-reflection.

By implementing these strategies, college students can pave the way for personal growth, resilience, and ultimately, a fulfilling college experience.

XXI. EMBRACING VULNERABILITY

Vulnerability, often seen as a weakness or a character flaw, is transformed into a powerful tool for personal growth and self-acceptance. Insecurity, which plagues the lives of countless individuals, can be conquered by embracing vulnerability and understanding its true nature. At its core, vulnerability is about opening oneself up to the possibility of being hurt, rejected, or disappointed. It requires individuals to shed their protective walls and allow themselves to be seen, heard, and felt authentically. This act of vulnerability, however, is not an invitation for others to take advantage of one's weaknesses, but rather an opportunity for growth and connection. Building upon the foundation of vulnerability, individuals can develop deeper levels of empathy, compassion, and understanding, leading to stronger interpersonal relationships. To embrace vulnerability, individuals must first confront and challenge their fears. Insecurity often stems from an innate fear of judgment or rejection, which prevents individuals from exposing their vulnerabilities to others. By challenging these fears and pushing past the discomfort, individuals can discover an unveiling sense of liberation. The fear of being judged or rejected loses its power when one realizes that even if faced with criticism or rejection, they are still worthy of love and belonging. . Vulnerability can be seen as a strength, as it demonstrates self-confidence and a willingness to take emotional risks. Embracing vulnerability also entails developing a sense of self-acceptance and self-compassion. Individuals become insecure when they compare themselves to others or hold themselves to unrealistic standards. By embracing vulnerability, individuals acknowledge and accept their own imperfections, acknowledging that they are no different from others who experience vulnerability. Rather than striving for perfection, individuals learn to be gentle with themselves and cultivate a sense of self-compassion. In doing so, they create an environment of acceptance that enables them to navigate vulnerability with authenticity and grace.

Vulnerability cultivates resilience, the ability to bounce back from adversity. By embracing vulnerability, individuals build emotional resilience by learning from experiences and embracing failures as opportunities for growth. Rather than succumbing to the fear of failure, individuals see it as an integral part of the journey towards success. Through their vulnerability, individuals develop a sense of courage to face obstacles head-on, knowing that their worth is not contingent upon their successes or failures. Embracing vulnerability is a fundamental aspect of overcoming insecurity. By challenging fears, developing self-acceptance and self-compassion, and cultivating resilience, individuals can transform vulnerability from a weakness into a source of strength. Although vulnerability requires individuals to open themselves up to potential pain or disappointment, it also presents an opportunity for growth, connection, and deeper understanding of oneself and others. In the twenty-first century, embracing vulnerability has emerged as a powerful tool for personal growth and self-acceptance, enabling individuals to overcome insecurity and live a more authentic and fulfilling life.

RECOGNIZING VULNERABILITY AS A STRENGTH, NOT A WEAKNESS

Many individuals view vulnerability as a negative trait, associating it with weakness and exposing oneself to potential harm or judgment. A shift in perspective is needed to understand vulnerability as a source of strength and an opportunity for personal growth. Vulnerability allows individuals to authentically connect with others, it promotes empathy and understanding, and it fosters resilience in the face of adversity.

First and foremost, vulnerability serves as a means for individuals to establish genuine connections with others. When one is vulnerable, they allow others to see their true selves, and this fosters authentic and deep connections. By sharing fears, doubts, and insecurities, individuals create an environment of trust and openness, where others can relate and offer support. In this way, vulnerability can be seen as an asset, providing an avenue for individuals to build strong relationships and cultivate a sense of belonging. Recognizing vulnerability as a strength enables individuals to develop empathy and understanding towards others. Insecurities stem from comparing oneself to others and harboring self-doubt. By realizing that everyone experiences vulnerability, individuals can have a greater appreciation for others' struggles and emotions. This heightened sense of empathy promotes compassion and nurtures a supportive environment where individuals can uplift one another. Understanding vulnerability in this light allows individuals to let go of judgment and instead offer understanding and assistance to those who are facing their own insecurities.

Vulnerability cultivates resilience and personal growth. It takes courage to be vulnerable, as it means facing fears and embracing uncertainty. This process creates a sense of resilience, enabling individuals to bounce back from setbacks and difficult situations. By acknowledging their vulnerabilities, individuals develop a deeper understanding of themselves and gain the tools to navigate life's challenges. This growth mindset allows individuals to view vulnerability not as a weakness, but as a catalyst for personal development. Recognizing vulnerability as a strength, not a weakness, is essential in overcoming insecurity. Vulnerability enhances connections by establishing genuine relationships and fostering a sense of belonging. It promotes empathy and understanding towards others, diminishing judgment and creating a supportive environment. Vulnerability cultivates resilience and personal growth by allowing individuals to face fears, embrace uncertainty, and develop a deep understanding of themselves. Thus, it is imperative to shift the perspective surrounding vulnerability, viewing it as a source of strength and an opportunity for personal growth, rather than a weakness to be avoided. By doing so, individuals can overcome insecurity and embrace their true selves, forming meaningful connections with others and thriving in the face of adversity.

SHARING INSECURITIES WITH TRUSTED INDIVIDUALS FOR SUPPORT

Once individuals have recognized their insecurities and taken steps towards self-acceptance, it is crucial for them to find a support system to share their vulnerabilities. Trusted individuals can offer a safe space to communicate these insecurities, fostering an atmosphere of understanding and empathy. This act of sharing not only allows individuals to unload their burdens, but also provides an opportunity for loved ones to offer words of encouragement and validation. The mere act of verbalizing these insecurities can provide a sense of relief, as it allows individuals to face their fears head-on and realize that they are not alone in their struggles. Trusted individuals can provide a fresh perspective on the situation, potentially offering solutions or coping mechanisms that the individual may not have considered. By sharing insecurities, individuals may also gain insights into their own emotions and thought processes, which can aid in the process of overcoming these insecurities. Trusted individuals can act as a source of motivation, reminding the individual of their strengths and achievements, thus boosting their self-esteem and self-worth. This can be especially important for individuals who are amidst a vulnerable period in their life, such as during a career transition or relationship difficulties.

In addition to benefiting the individual who is sharing their insecurities, this act can also strengthen existing relationships. By confiding in loved ones, individuals are forging deeper connections based on trust and vulnerability. This can enhance trust in the relationship, as well as foster a sense of reciprocity, as the trusted individual may feel more comfortable sharing their own insecurities in return. In turn, this reciprocation can lead to a deeper level of understanding and compassion within the relationship. Through this sharing, individuals can form a bond that is built on acceptance and the shared experience of vulnerability, which can ultimately contribute to increased emotional intimacy within the relationship. It is important to exercise caution when selecting trusted individuals to confide in. Seeking support from individuals who are non-judgmental, empathetic, and supportive is crucial. It is important to ensure that the trusted individuals are capable of providing the necessary emotional support and guidance, rather than exacerbating insecurities further. While it is tempting to resort to sharing insecurities with a large group of individuals, it is imperative to prioritize quality over quantity. A select few trusted individuals who possess the emotional capacity to support and uplift the individual can be far more beneficial. Confidentiality is also of utmost importance, as individuals should feel safe in the knowledge that their vulnerabilities will be protected. Sharing insecurities with trusted individuals can be a vital step in overcoming insecurity. By providing a safe space for individuals to share their vulnerabilities, loved ones can offer understanding, encouragement, and fresh perspectives. This act not only aids in relieving the burden of these insecurities but also strengthens relationships through trust, vulnerability, and emotional intimacy. Choosing trusted individuals wisely and ensuring confidentiality is maintained are key aspects of this process. The act of sharing insecurities can be transformative, leading individuals towards self-acceptance and growth.

CONNECTING WITH OTHERS ON A DEEPER AND MORE AUTHENTIC LEVEL

Insecurity often stems from a fear of judgment or rejection by others, and so building genuine connections can help to alleviate these concerns. One way to foster deeper connections is through active listening. By truly hearing and understanding what others are saying, we can establish rapport and trust, confirming that our thoughts and feelings matter. This validation has a powerful effect on our sense of self-worth. Sharing our own vulnerabilities and being open about our insecurities can create a safe and supportive environment for others to reciprocate. This vulnerability enables us to bond over shared experiences and emotions, reinforcing the realization that we are not alone in our struggles. Striving for meaningful connections requires us to practice empathy. By putting ourselves in the shoes of others and trying to understand their perspectives, we can better connect with them on an emotional level. This empathy allows us to validate their feelings and provides a solid foundation for a deeper connection. Maintaining healthy boundaries in relationships is essential to feeling secure. Setting boundaries helps us protect ourselves emotionally and establishes a sense of self-respect. When we communicate our boundaries effectively, we signal to others that we value ourselves and expect to be treated with dignity. This clarity fosters a sense of security within relationships. Engaging in activities that foster shared interests and values can deepen connections. Pursuing shared hobbies or participating in group activities provides a common ground where we can connect with others on a deeper level. Through shared experiences, we can build meaningful connections with those who share our passions and values, reinforcing our sense of belonging. Embracing vulnerability and practicing self-compassion are key to developing authentic connections. Accepting ourselves as imperfect beings and acknowledging that it is okay to make mistakes allows us to be more genuine with others. By practicing self-compassion, we become more accepting and forgiving of our flaws, making it easier to connect with others without the fear of judgment. Overcoming insecurity requires developing deeper and more authentic connections with others. This can be achieved through active listening, sharing vulnerabilities, practicing empathy, setting healthy boundaries, engaging in shared activities, and embracing vulnerability. When we foster these connections, we not only build a sense of belonging and support but also gain a better understanding of our own self-worth. Our interpersonal relationships have a profound impact on our self-perception, and by cultivating deeper connections, we can ultimately overcome insecurity and develop a greater sense of confidence and acceptance within ourselves. One of the most common yet underestimated issues that individuals may face is insecurity. Insecurity can manifest in various aspects of life, including relationships, academics, and personal growth. Overcoming insecurity is crucial for personal development and overall well-being. To begin with, introspection is an essential step on the path to overcoming insecurity. It entails examining oneself and identifying the root causes of one's insecurities. For instance, past experiences, societal pressures, or even unrealistic expectations can contribute to feelings of insecurity. By reflecting on these factors, individuals can gain a better understanding of themselves and their insecurities, which in turn enables them to confront and overcome them. Seeking external help and support is another vital aspect of overcoming insecurity. Whether it be confiding in a trusted friend, family member, or seeking professional guidance through therapy, gaining outside perspective and support can provide invaluable insights and encouragement. Engaging in positive self-talk and challenging negative thoughts can significantly aid in alleviating insecurity. Negative self-talk perpetuates feelings of inadequacy and self-doubt and hampers personal growth. Consciously replacing negative thoughts with positive affirmations can help rewire the mind and foster a healthier self-image. Setting achievable goals and celebrating small milestones can boost self-confidence and diminish feelings of insecurity. By breaking down larger goals into smaller, manageable tasks, individuals can experience a sense of accomplishment, reinforcing the belief in their capabilities. This method empowers individuals to overcome their insecurity by proving to themselves that they are capable and competent. Pursuing activities that challenge one's comfort zone can be an effective strategy for overcoming insecurity. Stepping out of one's comfort zone promotes personal growth and resilience, enabling individuals to build confidence and reduce insecurities. Engaging in activities such as public speaking, attending networking events, or learning new skills pushes individuals beyond their self-imposed limitations and fosters a sense of personal achievement. Practicing self-care and cultivating self-acceptance are fundamental elements in overcoming insecurity. Taking care of one's physical, mental, and emotional well-being is essential for building resilience and developing a positive self-image. Engaging in activities that promote relaxation, such as yoga or meditation, can help manage stress and anxiety, contributing to a greater sense of self-assurance. Embracing one's flaws and imperfections with self-compassion allows individuals to accept themselves wholly and unconditionally. By recognizing that nobody is perfect and that imperfections are part of human nature, individuals can alleviate the harsh judgments they impose upon themselves, leading to increased self-esteem and diminished insecurity. To conclude, overcoming insecurity is a complex yet crucial journey towards self-improvement and personal growth. Through introspection, seeking support, engaging in positive self-talk, setting achievable goals, stepping out of comfort zones, practicing self-care, and cultivating self-acceptance, individuals can overcome their insecurities and embrace a more confident and fulfilling life. By embracing these strategies, individuals can transform their insecurities into strengths and embark on a journey of personal empowerment and happiness.

XXII. TAKING PERSONAL RESPONSIBILITY

Insecurity often stems from a lack of self-belief and confidence in one's abilities and decisions. By acknowledging and accepting personal responsibility for our actions and choices, we empower ourselves to make positive changes in our lives. Taking personal responsibility means recognizing that our actions and decisions have consequences and that we are responsible for the outcomes. It requires us to accept that we have the power to shape our lives and determine our own happiness. By taking personal responsibility, we can break free from the cycle of insecurity and start building a more fulfilling and confident life.

One way to take personal responsibility is to reflect on our choices and actions. Instead of blaming external factors or other people for our mistakes or failures, we need to look inward and ask ourselves what role we played in the situation. This self-reflection is not meant to incite self-blame but rather to foster growth and learning. By acknowledging our own contributions, we can identify areas where we need to improve and take action to make positive changes. This self-awareness is essential for personal growth and the development of confidence. Another aspect of taking personal responsibility is owning up to our mistakes and apologizing when necessary. Insecurities often arise from a fear of judgment or rejection, but by accepting our faults and taking responsibility for them, we show humility and integrity. Apologizing demonstrates that we understand the impact of our actions on others and are willing to make amends. This not only helps repair relationships but also allows us to grow and learn from our mistakes. By taking ownership of our behavior, we break down the walls of insecurity and build trust and respect in our interactions with others.

Taking personal responsibility involves setting goals and taking action towards achieving them. Insecurity often stems from a lack of direction and purpose in life. By setting clear goals and taking intentional steps towards achieving them, we gain a sense of control and direction. This process allows us to focus on our strengths and areas of growth, leading to increased self-confidence and a reduction in insecurities. It is important to remember that progress is not always linear and setbacks are a part of the journey. By taking ownership of our goals and actions, we can persevere through challenges and overcome obstacles, further fostering a sense of personal responsibility and confidence in ourselves. Taking personal responsibility is a fundamental step in overcoming insecurity. By reflecting on our choices, owning up to our mistakes, and taking action towards our goals, we empower ourselves to break free from the cycle of insecurity. Personal responsibility allows us to acknowledge our power to shape our lives and take control of our happiness. Through this process, we develop self-belief and confidence, paving the way for personal growth and a more fulfilling life.

OWNING MISTAKES AND TAKING ACTION TO RECTIFY THEM

Insecurity often stems from a fear of making mistakes or being judged for them. By acknowledging our mistakes and taking responsibility for them, we can break free from this cycle of insecurity. Owning our mistakes requires humility and self-awareness. It means recognizing that we are not perfect and that we are capable of making errors. Rather than trying to hide or deny our mistakes, we should face them head-on and take responsibility for the consequences. This can be a challenging process as it requires admitting our shortcomings and facing potential judgment from others. Nevertheless, it is an essential step towards personal growth and developing a sense of self-confidence. Owning mistakes also involves understanding the impact our actions may have on others. When we recognize that our mistakes can negatively affect those around us, we become more compelled to rectify them. Taking action to rectify mistakes demonstrates accountability and a commitment to personal and professional integrity. It requires identifying the steps needed to correct the situation and following through with them. This may involve apologizing to those affected by our mistakes, offering restitution, or implementing changes to avoid similar errors in the future. By taking active steps to rectify our mistakes, we not only show others that we genuinely care about the consequences of our actions, but we also prove to ourselves that we can overcome our insecurities. Owning mistakes and taking action to rectify them fosters a culture of learning and growth. When we are open about our mistakes, it creates an environment where others feel comfortable acknowledging their own errors. This promotes a sense of empathy and understanding, as we realize that everyone is susceptible to making mistakes. Taking action to rectify mistakes allows us to learn from our experiences and grow as individuals. Each mistake becomes an opportunity for personal development and gaining wisdom. By facing our mistakes head-on, we develop resilience and become better equipped to handle future challenges. Insecurity often hinders our ability to take risks or pursue new opportunities. When we own our mistakes, we become more confident in our abilities to navigate future challenges. By understanding that mistakes are a natural part of life, we can let go of the fear of failure and embrace new opportunities with a sense of self-assurance. Owning mistakes and taking action to rectify them is a vital step in overcoming insecurity. It requires humility, self-awareness, and a commitment to personal growth. By owning our mistakes, we break free from the cycle of insecurity and gain self-confidence. Taking action to rectify mistakes promotes accountability, fosters a culture of learning and growth, and equips us with resilience to face future challenges. By embracing mistakes as opportunities for growth, we can overcome our insecurities and live more fulfilling lives.

AVOIDING BLAME-SHIFTING OR VICTIM MENTALITY

Blame-shifting occurs when individuals refuse to take responsibility for their actions or choices and instead point fingers at others. This behavior stems from a victim mentality, which is characterized by a belief that one is always at the mercy of external circumstances or the actions of others. By avoiding blame-shifting and victim mentality, individuals can regain control over their lives and develop a more secure sense of self.

Blame-shifting is a defense mechanism that people often employ to protect their ego. It allows them to avoid confronting their own mistakes or shortcomings by blaming others for their problems or failures. This behavior is detrimental to personal growth and only perpetuates feelings of insecurity.

Taking responsibility for one's actions and choices is an essential aspect of adulthood and maturity. It empowers individuals to learn from their mistakes and make healthier decisions in the future, fostering personal development and a stronger self-image. Similarly, a victim mentality can be a significant barrier to overcoming insecurity. Those who adopt this mindset believe that they are constantly subjected to unfair treatment or circumstances beyond their control, which fuels feelings of helplessness and dependency. While it is true that external factors can affect our lives, allowing oneself to continually adopt the role of a victim hinders personal growth and self-confidence. Instead of dwelling on past traumas or difficult situations, individuals must recognize their ability to take control of their own lives and make positive changes. This shift in mindset allows for greater autonomy and resilience in the face of adversity.

Overcoming blame-shifting and victim mentality requires a shift in perspective and an active commitment to personal growth. Individuals must be willing to acknowledge their role in the events that have shaped their lives and take responsibility for their actions. This can be a challenging process, as it involves confronting personal insecurities and facing the fear of failure or judgment. By embracing accountability, individuals can break free from the cycle of blame and victimhood and establish a stronger sense of self. Developing self-compassion and empathy can aid in the process of overcoming blame-shifting and victim mentality. By acknowledging one's own vulnerabilities and experiences, individuals can cultivate a greater understanding and empathy towards others. This shift in mindset encourages individuals to view challenges as opportunities for growth and to approach adversity with resilience and determination. Avoiding blame-shifting and victim mentality is essential in overcoming insecurity. By taking responsibility for one's actions and choices, individuals can regain control over their lives and foster personal growth. It is crucial to let go of the victim mindset and instead embrace a proactive and empowered approach to life. Through self-compassion, empathy, and a commitment to personal development, individuals can overcome insecurity and cultivate a stronger sense of self.

EMPOWERING ONESELF BY TAKING CONTROL OF ONE'S ACTIONS AND CHOICES

Insecurity often stems from a lack of confidence in oneself, leading individuals to feel powerless and limited in their capabilities. By actively taking charge of their actions and choices, individuals can regain a sense of control and agency over their lives. One way to achieve this is by setting clear goals and actively working towards them. By identifying the areas in which they feel insecure and developing a plan to improve in those areas, individuals can take concrete steps towards personal growth and development. This process not only increases their self-esteem but also allows them to take pride in their accomplishments, thus challenging their feelings of insecurity.

Engaging in self-reflection and introspection can be instrumental in empowering oneself. By reflecting on past experiences and examining the root causes of their insecurities, individuals can gain valuable insights into themselves and their patterns of thinking. This awareness enables them to question self-destructive beliefs and replace them with more positive and empowering ones. It opens up the possibility of self-forgiveness and self-compassion, which are essential components of personal growth. Taking control of one's actions and choices involves actively practicing self-care. Engaging in activities that bring joy and fulfillment, prioritizing physical and mental well-being, and setting healthy boundaries are all crucial aspects of self-care that allow individuals to nurture themselves and build resilience. By investing time and energy in self-care, individuals create a foundation of strength and stability that helps them navigate challenges and setbacks with greater confidence. Making informed choices and asserting oneself in various aspects of life can greatly contribute to empowerment. This can be achieved by expressing one's needs, desires, and boundaries clearly and respectfully in personal relationships and professional settings. By advocating for oneself and actively participating in decision-making processes, individuals assert their worth and affirm their place in the world. Actively seeking out opportunities for growth, learning, and skill development can further empower individuals. This can involve enrolling in courses or attending workshops, reading books, or seeking guidance from mentors or support networks. By expanding their knowledge and skill base, individuals not only enhance their abilities but also deepen their sense of self-worth and their belief in their capacity to overcome challenges. Empowering oneself by taking control of one's actions and choices is a transformative process that requires commitment, resilience, and self-reflection. By setting goals, engaging in self-care, practicing self-reflection, making informed choices, and seeking growth opportunities, individuals can break free from insecurities and develop an empowering mindset. This journey allows individuals to challenge limiting beliefs, build confidence, and embrace their unique strengths, leading to a greater sense of authentic self and a more fulfilling and empowered life.

One of the most important steps in overcoming insecurity is to develop a strong sense of self-worth. Insecurity often stems from a lack of confidence in one's own abilities or worthiness. To combat this, individuals must engage in self-reflection and actively work towards building a positive self-image. One effective strategy is to identify and challenge negative self-talk. This requires paying close attention to the thoughts and beliefs that contribute to feelings of insecurity and questioning their validity. For example, if one constantly tells themselves that they are not good enough, they need to critically examine whether this belief is based on evidence or if it is merely an unfounded assumption. By challenging these negative thoughts and replacing them with more positive and realistic ones, individuals can begin to shift their mindset towards self-acceptance and appreciation. Another helpful approach is to set achievable goals and actively work towards accomplishing them. By setting small, attainable goals, individuals can experience a sense of accomplishment and increase their self-confidence. As they continue to achieve these goals, their belief in their own abilities grows, leading to a more secure sense of self. Seeking out support from others can greatly aid in overcoming insecurity. Trusted friends, family members, or mentors can provide valuable insight, encouragement, and perspective. They can help to challenge self-doubt and provide reassurance during difficult times. Joining support groups or seeking professional help, such as therapy or counseling, can also be beneficial. These resources offer a safe space to explore insecurities, gain new insights, and learn coping mechanisms. Another effective strategy for overcoming insecurity is to practice self-care. Engaging in activities that promote physical, mental, and emotional well-being can foster a greater sense of self-esteem and security. This might include exercise, healthy eating, engaging in hobbies, or practicing Mindfulness and self-compassion. Taking time for self-care can improve one's overall outlook on life and provide a strong foundation for self-confidence. It is important to remember that overcoming insecurity is a journey that takes time and patience. It is normal to experience setbacks, doubts, and moments of insecurity along the way. By implementing these strategies consistently and persistently, individuals can start to transform their mindset and build a foundation of self-worth. Through self-reflection, challenging negative self-talk, setting achievable goals, seeking support, practicing self-care, and maintaining a mindset of growth and self-acceptance, individuals can overcome their insecurities and thrive. By developing a strong sense of self-worth, individuals can embrace their unique qualities and confidently navigate the challenges of life.

XXIII. CELEBRATING PERSONAL GROWTH

As individuals, we often find ourselves doubting our abilities, constantly comparing ourselves to others, and feeling like we are not measuring up to societal standards. Taking the time to acknowledge and celebrate our personal growth allows us to break free from the chains of self-doubt and insecurity. By recognizing our accomplishments, big or small, we empower ourselves to continue growing and striving for greatness.

When we celebrate personal growth, we shift our mindset from focusing on our flaws and weaknesses to acknowledging our strengths and achievements. Insecurity often stems from a lack of self-confidence, and this can hinder our progress in various areas of life, such as relationships, academic pursuits, and career paths. Celebrating personal growth helps build our self-esteem and reminds us that we are capable and worthy of success. This celebration acts as a powerful motivator, encouraging us to continue working towards our goals, despite any setbacks or obstacles we may face. Celebrating personal growth provides us with a sense of validation and fulfillment. In a world that is constantly demanding perfection and success, it is easy to forget that progress is a journey rather than a destination. When we take the time to recognize our progress, we acknowledge the effort and dedication we have put into ourselves. This validation serves as a reminder that we are on the right path and that our growth is significant and worthy of celebration. Celebrating personal growth allows us to experience a sense of fulfillment as we reflect upon how far we have come in our personal development. This fulfillment acts as a source of motivation and fuel to continue evolving and striving for self-improvement. Celebrating personal growth helps us appreciate the value of our experiences and the lessons we have learned along the way. Insecurity often causes us to underestimate ourselves and our abilities, leading us to overlook the lessons and growth opportunities that come from our challenges and failures. By celebrating personal growth, we honor these experiences, both positive and negative. We recognize that every experience, good or bad, has contributed to our growth and has made us who we are today. This appreciation not only boosts our self-confidence but also encourages us to view setbacks as opportunities for growth rather than reasons to give up.

Celebrating personal growth is a crucial step in overcoming insecurity and building self-confidence. By shifting our focus from our flaws to our accomplishments, we empower ourselves to continue growing and striving for greatness. This celebration not only validates our progress but also provides a sense of fulfillment and motivation to keep pushing forward. By appreciating the value of our experiences, we embrace the growth opportunities that come from challenges and failures. Celebrating personal growth allows us to break free from the chains of self-doubt and insecurity, ultimately leading us to a more confident and fulfilling life.

REFLECTING ON PROGRESS MADE IN OVERCOMING INSECURITIES

In my journey of dealing with my own insecurities, I have come a long way, and I am proud of the progress I have made. Initially, I was consumed by self-doubt and constantly compared myself to those around me. This led to a constant feeling of inadequacy and a distorted perception of my own worth. Through self-reflection and self-compassion, I have been able to challenge and overcome these insecurities. One significant progress I have made is in embracing my uniqueness. I have realized that everyone has their own strengths and weaknesses, and there is no need to compare myself to others. By focusing on my own abilities and talents, I have been able to appreciate my individuality and recognize my worth. This shift in mindset has not only boosted my self-confidence but has also allowed me to recognize and celebrate the achievements of others without feeling overshadowed or threatened. Another essential aspect of my progress is in challenging negative self-talk and cultivating a positive mindset. In the past, I would constantly criticize myself and ruminate over my mistakes, which only exacerbated my insecurities. I have learned that by replacing negative thoughts with positive affirmations, I can rewire my brain and nurture a more compassionate inner voice. This conscious effort to practice self-kindness has not only improved my self-esteem but has also enabled me to approach challenges with a growth mindset and view failure as an opportunity for growth rather than a reflection of my worth. I have made significant strides in accepting and embracing vulnerability. Insecurities often stem from a fear of being judged or rejected. I have come to understand that vulnerability is not a weakness but a strength. By allowing myself to be vulnerable and opening up to others, I have formed deeper and more meaningful connections. This has not only helped me create a support system but has also shown me that vulnerability allows for genuine connections and fosters empathy and understanding. I have realized that overcoming insecurities is an ongoing process. It requires continuous self-re flection, self-care, and self-compassion. There are days when I still struggle with self-doubt, but I have learned to be patient with myself and acknowledge that progress is not always linear. Celebrating small victories along the way has been instrumental in sustaining my progress and maintaining a positive mindset.

The progress I have made in overcoming insecurities has been transformative. Embracing my uniqueness, challenging negative self-talk, accepting vulnerability, and acknowledging that progress is an ongoing journey have all contributed to my personal growth and self-acceptance. While insecurities may still surface at times, I am confident in my ability to overcome them and live a life that is authentic and true to myself. Reflecting on the milestones I have achieved in this journey fills me with a sense of empowerment and encourages me to continue striving for growth and self-acceptance.

ACKNOWLEDGING AND CELEBRATING PERSONAL ACHIEVEMENTS

In a society that values external validation and constant comparison, individuals often find themselves questioning their worth and abilities. It is important to counter this mindset by acknowledging and celebrating personal achievements. This process involves recognizing one's own accomplishments, no matter how big or small, and giving oneself credit for them. When individuals learn to appreciate the progress they have made and the goals they have achieved, they can begin to develop a sense of self-worth that is not reliant on external factors. Acknowledging personal achievements is a powerful tool in combating insecurity because it allows individuals to shift their focus from their perceived shortcomings to their strengths. By recognizing their accomplishments, individuals gain a better understanding of their skills and values, leading to increased self-confidence. This shift in mindset enables individuals to approach new challenges with a more positive attitude and the belief that they are capable of overcoming obstacles. When people celebrate their personal achievements, they reinforce the notion that their efforts have not gone unnoticed. This recognition can serve as a source of motivation and encouragement, propelling individuals to continue striving for success.

Celebrating personal achievements can help individuals develop a healthier perspective on failure. Insecurity often stems from the fear of failure and the belief that one's mistakes define their worth. By acknowledging and celebrating personal achievements, individuals begin to view failure as an opportunity for growth rather than a reflection of their capabilities. Through this process, they realize that failure is a natural part of the learning curve and that it does not diminish their value as individuals. This mindset shift promotes resilience and a willingness to take risks, as individuals understand that their self-worth is not contingent on external outcomes. Celebrating personal achievements fosters a sense of empowerment and autonomy. When individuals recognize and celebrate their own accomplishments, they take ownership of their successes and validate their own efforts. This self-validation is liberating, as it allows individuals to define their worth based on their own standards rather than seeking approval from others. This newfound sense of empowerment enables individuals to pursue their goals and dreams with conviction and determination, regardless of external validation or societal expectations. Acknowledging and celebrating personal achievements plays a pivotal role in overcoming insecurity. By recognizing one's own accomplishments, individuals gain a better understanding of their strengths and values, leading to increased self-confidence and resilience. Celebrating personal achievements helps individuals develop a healthier perspective on failure, viewing it as an opportunity for growth rather than a reflection of their worth. This process fosters a sense of empowerment and autonomy, enabling individuals to pursue their goals and dreams with conviction. Through the practice of acknowledging and celebrating personal achievements, individuals can overcome insecurity and develop a strong sense of self-worth that is resilient to external influences.

USING MILESTONES AS MOTIVATION FOR FURTHER GROWTH

Setting milestones is a crucial aspect of personal development as it allows individuals to track their progress and celebrate their achievements. These milestones serve as reminders of the progress made and can boost self-confidence and motivation to continue moving forward. When overcoming insecurity, setting small achievable goals can provide a sense of accomplishment and increase one's belief in their abilities. For instance, if an individual struggles with public speaking due to insecurity, they can set a milestone of speaking in front of a small group of friends or family members. Once this milestone is achieved, the individual can gain confidence in their speaking abilities and gradually progress towards speaking in front of larger audiences. By leveraging milestones, individuals can break down their insecurities into smaller, more manageable tasks, making the path to personal growth seem less daunting.

Milestones not only provide a sense of achievement but also act as indicators of personal advancement. By evaluating progress through milestones, individuals can assess their strengths and weaknesses, identify areas for improvement, and devise strategies to address them. Regularly reviewing progress against these milestones enables individuals to reflect on their growth, appreciate how far they have come, and identify areas that still need development. This self-reflection is essential as it allows individuals to address any lingering insecurities and work towards further growth. For example, an individual struggling with body image issues may set a milestone of improving their fitness level. As they work towards this milestone and notice changes in their physical appearance and overall well-being, their confidence and self-esteem may improve, leading to a reduction in insecurity. In addition to personal growth, milestones can also foster a sense of community and support. Sharing milestones with others can create a support network that provides encouragement, advice, and motivation. This sense of community is essential in overcoming insecurity as it helps individuals realize that they are not alone in their struggles and that others have faced similar challenges. Receiving feedback or validation from others when milestones are achieved can reinforce an individual's belief in their capabilities and increase their motivation to conquer insecurities. Through the shared experience of setting and achieving milestones, individuals can form stronger connections with others, enhancing their overall sense of belonging and self-worth. Using milestones as motivation for further growth is a powerful tool in overcoming insecurities. By setting achievable goals and celebrating achievements, individuals can boost their self-confidence and motivation to continue working towards personal growth. Milestones not only provide a sense of accomplishment but also act as indicators of progress, allowing individuals to evaluate their strengths, weaknesses, and areas for improvement. Sharing milestones with others fosters a sense of community and support, enhancing an individual's belief in their abilities and reducing insecurity. By utilizing milestones effectively, individuals can break down their insecurities into manageable tasks, make significant progress in personal growth, and ultimately overcome their insecurities.

The topic of insecurity is one that affects many individuals on various levels. Insecurity can stem from a multitude of sources, including personal experiences, societal pressures, and the comparison to others. To overcome insecurity, it is essential to understand its roots, make a conscious effort to challenge negative thoughts and beliefs, and foster self-acceptance and self-love. Insecurity often arises from personal experiences that have shaken an individual's confidence and self-es teem. Traumatic events, failures, or rejection can leave deep emotional scars, making it difficult to believe in oneself. To overcome insecurity, it is crucial to identify and address the underlying causes. This may involve seeking therapy or counseling to work through past traumas, gaining a deeper understanding of individual strengths and weaknesses, and learning from past mistakes rather than dwelling on them. By acknowledging and processing these experiences, individuals can gradually rebuild their confidence and reduce their insecurities. Another factor that contributes to insecurity is the societal pressure to conform to certain ideals. The media, society, and even peer groups often dictate what is considered attractive, successful, or worthy. Constant comparison to these standards can lead to feelings of inadequacy and self-doubt. To overcome this, individuals need to challenge these societal norms and redefine their own measure of success and worthiness. Recognizing that everyone has their unique strengths and qualities helps in appreciating oneself and focusing on personal growth rather than chasing external validation. Challenging negative thoughts and beliefs is another crucial aspect of overcoming insecurity. Insecure individuals often have an inner dialogue filled with self-doubt, criticism, and negative self-perception. This internal narrative can greatly influence one's self-esteem and confidence levels. To change this narrative, individuals must actively identify and challenge their negative thoughts. This could involve reframing negative statements, focusing on positive aspects, and practicing self-compassion. Affirmations and positive self-talk can also be powerful tools in replacing negative beliefs with more empowering ones. Fostering self-acceptance and self-love is fundamental in overcoming insecurity. Accepting oneself fully, flaws and all, is a significant step towards building self-esteem. This involves embracing one's strengths, accepting limitations, and celebrating individuality. Developing self-love requires nurturing a healthy relationship with oneself, prioritizing self-care, and practicing self-compassion. Treating oneself as a friend, rather than a critic, can create a nurturing environment in which self-confidence can flourish. Overcoming insecurity begins with understanding its roots and addressing personal experiences that may have contributed to it. Challenging societal norms, negative thoughts, and beliefs is essential in developing a more positive self-perception. Fostering self-acceptance and self-love creates a foundation for building confidence and reducing insecurity. While overcoming insecurity can be a gradual process, it is an important journey towards living a more fulfilling and authentic life.

XXIV. EMBRACING THE JOURNEY

Insecurity is an all-encompassing feeling that can consume a person's mindset and hinder personal growth. It is a hurdle that must be overcome in order to lead a fulfilling life. Overcoming insecurity is not a linear process, but rather a journey. This journey involves self-reflection, acceptance, and embracing the unknown. Self-reflection is the first step towards overcoming insecurity. Taking the time to analyze one's thoughts and beliefs allows individuals to gain a deeper understanding of their own insecurities. This process involves questioning the origins of these insecurities and examining the underlying thoughts and emotions that fuel them. Self-reflection requires individuals to be honest with themselves, facing their fears head-on. By exploring the roots of their insecurities, individuals can begin to unravel the negative thought patterns that keep them trapped in a cycle of self-doubt. Acceptance is another crucial aspect of the journey towards overcoming insecurity. It involves acknowledging that insecurities are a part of being human and that everyone experiences them to some extent. Acceptance is not about resigning oneself to a life of insecurity but rather recognizing that it is possible to move beyond it. This acknowledgment allows individuals to let go of perfectionism and unrealistic expectations they may have set for themselves. Acceptance involves being gentle and patient with oneself, understanding that progress may be slow at times, but every step forward is significant. Perhaps the most challenging aspect of this journey is embracing the unknown. Insecurity often thrives on uncertainty and the fear of the unfamiliar. To overcome it, individuals must learn to embrace the unknown and step outside their comfort zones. This may involve taking risks, trying new experiences, and challenging oneself in various aspects of life. Embracing the unknown requires individuals to trust in their abilities and believe that they are capable of navigating through uncertainty. It involves cultivating resilience and a willingness to learn from failures and setbacks. By embracing the unknown, individuals open themselves up to new possibilities and opportunities for growth. The journey towards overcoming insecurity is not a solitary one. It requires support from others and the creation of a strong support system. Connecting with like-minded individuals who understand and empathize with one's struggles can be instrumental in the process of overcoming insecurity. Surrounding oneself with positive influences and seeking guidance from mentors or therapists can provide valuable insights and help individuals gain a fresh perspective on their insecurities. Sharing one's journey with others can be empowering, as it fosters a sense of community and reminds individuals that they are not alone in their struggles. Overcoming insecurity is a challenging but worthwhile journey. It requires self-reflection, acceptance, and embracing the unknown. By delving deep into the origins of insecurities, individuals can gain a better understanding of themselves and begin to challenge negative thought patterns. Acceptance allows individuals to let go of perfectionism and unrealistic expectations while embracing the unknown encourages them to step outside their comfort zones and explore new possibilities. Nonetheless, this journey is not an isolated one and requires the support and understanding of others. With determination and resilience, individuals can navigate through insecurity and embark on a path towards self-acceptance and personal growth.

RECOGNIZING THAT OVERCOMING INSECURITY IS A LIFELONG PROCESS

Recognizing that overcoming insecurity is a lifelong process is crucial for personal growth and development. Insecurity is a common human emotion that often stems from various factors such as childhood experiences, societal pressures, or past failures. It manifests itself in different ways, such as low self-esteem, self-doubt, and a fear of judgment or rejection. Overcoming these insecurities requires a multifaceted approach that involves self-reflection, challenging limiting beliefs, and building a strong support system. It is important to understand that this journey is not a one-time event but rather a continual process that requires ongoing effort and attention.

One of the first steps in overcoming insecurity is recognizing its presence in our lives. Insecurity can often be so deeply ingrained that we may not even be aware of its presence or how it affects our actions and decisions. By acknowledging our insecurities, we can begin to explore their origins and understand the underlying causes. This self-reflection allows us to gain insight into our thought patterns and behaviors, which is essential in breaking free from the cycle of insecurity. Challenging limiting beliefs is another integral aspect of overcoming insecurity. Insecurities are often rooted in negative self-perceptions and distorted thinking patterns. These beliefs can hold us back from reaching our true potential and hinder personal growth. By questioning and challenging these beliefs, we can start to reframe our thoughts in a more positive and realistic manner. This may involve seeking professional help or engaging in self-help practices such as affirmations or cognitive-behavioral therapy. As we change our mindset and challenge our limiting beliefs, we can gradually build confidence and self-assurance.

Building a strong support system is instrumental in the journey of overcoming insecurity. Surrounding ourselves with positive and supportive individuals who believe in our abilities can boost our self-esteem and provide invaluable encouragement. These individuals can offer a different perspective, provide constructive feedback, and empower us to confront our insecurities head-on. Participating in support groups or seeking guidance from mentors can offer a sense of belonging and understanding, knowing that we are not alone in our struggles.

While these steps are essential, it is imperative to understand that overcoming insecurity is not a linear process. It is not a destination but rather a continual journey. Insecurities may resurface at different points in our lives, triggered by new experiences or challenges. Recognizing this ebb and flow is crucial in maintaining self-awareness and actively working towards self-improvement. By accepting that insecurity may never be completely eradicated, we can focus on developing resilience and coping mechanisms to navigate moments of vulnerability.

Recognizing that overcoming insecurity is a lifelong process is essential for personal growth and development. By acknowledging its presence, challenging limiting beliefs, and building a strong support system, individuals can begin to break free from the cycle of insecurity. It is crucial to understand that this journey requires ongoing effort and attention.

By embracing the fact that insecurity is not a destination but a continuous journey, individuals can develop the resilience and coping mechanisms necessary to navigate life's challenges and embrace their true potential.

BEING PATIENT AND COMPASSIONATE TOWARD ONESELF DURING SETBACKS

Insecurities often stem from a lack of confidence and self-belief, which can be reinforced by setbacks and failures. When faced with a setback, it is all too easy to succumb to self-criticism and negative self-talk, further exacerbating one's insecurities. Adopting a patient and compassionate mindset toward oneself can help break this cycle. Patience allows individuals to recognize that setbacks are a natural part of the learning process and that success rarely happens overnight. It takes time to develop new skills and overcome challenges. By being patient, individuals are more likely to stick with their goals and persevere through obstacles. Compassion toward oneself is essential in fostering a healthier self-image. Instead of berating oneself for not meeting expectations, showing compassion means treating oneself with kindness and understanding. Viewing setbacks as opportunities for growth rather than personal failures can help alleviate feelings of insecurity and foster a more positive outlook. Compassion also involves acknowledging one's emotions and validating their significance. It is natural to feel disappointed, frustrated, or discouraged when faced with a setback, and acknowledging these emotions rather than suppressing them can lead to healthier coping mechanisms.

In addition to patience and compassion, adopting a growth mindset is also essential in overcoming insecurities. A growth mindset is the belief that abilities and intelligence can be developed through dedication and hard work. Embracing this mindset encourages individuals to view setbacks as learning experiences rather than indicators of their worth or ability. Instead of accepting failure as the end result, a growth mindset fosters resilience and a determination to keep trying. It allows individuals to recognize that setbacks are not permanent, and with effort and perseverance, they can overcome challenges. By believing in their ability to learn and grow, individuals can begin to challenge their insecurities and build their self-confidence.

While being patient, compassionate, and maintaining a growth mindset are vital in overcoming insecurities, it is also important to seek support from others. Building a strong support system can provide individuals with encouragement, guidance, and perspective during challenging times. Whether it be friends, family, or mentors, surrounding oneself with positive influences can help reinforce feelings of self-worth and counteract the negative self-talk often associated with insecurities. Seeking professional help, such as therapy or counseling, can provide individuals with specialized tools and strategies for overcoming insecurities and building self-esteem. Sometimes, it is beneficial to have an objective perspective and expertise to guide one through the process of self-improvement and building resilience. Being patient and compassionate toward oneself during setbacks is crucial for overcoming insecurities. By adopting a growth mindset, individuals can view setbacks as opportunities for growth, as opposed to personal failures. Seeking support from others is also important, as it can provide encouragement and guidance throughout the journey of self-improvement. Overcoming one's insecurities requires a combination of self-compassion, resilience, and a belief in one's ability to grow and develop.

EMBRACING THE CONTINUOUS JOURNEY OF SELF-DISCOVERY AND GROWTH

Insecurity often stems from a lack of self-awareness and a fear of change. By embracing the continuous journey of self-discovery and growth, individuals can gain a better understanding of themselves, their strengths, and their potential. This journey involves being open to new experiences, exploring different perspectives, and challenging one's comfort zone. It requires a willingness to examine one's values, beliefs, and motivations, and to question preconceived notions. Self-reflection and introspection are crucial components of this journey, as they enable individuals to gain insight into their thoughts, emotions, and behaviors. The process of self-discovery and growth is not a linear path but a continuous one. It involves a series of moments of self-reflection and self-evaluation. Through these moments, individuals can identify their strengths, weaknesses, and areas for improvement. By acknowledging and accepting these aspects of themselves, individuals can begin to develop a sense of self-confidence and security. This process also involves understanding one's values and aligning actions with these values. In doing so, individuals can foster a sense of integrity and authenticity, which can further enhance their self-esteem and sense of self-worth. Embracing the continuous journey of self-discovery and growth also requires a willingness to take risks and embrace uncertainty. Growth often occurs outside of one's comfort zone, and individuals must be willing to step into the unknown in order to discover their full potential. This may involve pursuing new opportunities, trying new activities, or engaging in challenging conversations. By pushing past fears and limitations, individuals can expand their horizons and gain a greater understanding of themselves and the world around them. Embracing the continuous journey of self-discovery and growth involves seeking feedback and learning from others. It can be difficult to gain an objective view of oneself, and the perspectives of others can provide valuable insight and guidance. This may involve seeking feedback from mentors, peers, or even engaging in therapy or counseling. By actively seeking feedback and reflecting on it, individuals can gain a more accurate understanding of their strengths and areas for improvement. This process of self-reflection and feedback can help individuals develop a growth mindset, where challenges and setbacks are seen as opportunities for learning and growth.

Embracing the continuous journey of self-discovery and growth is crucial in overcoming insecurity. By engaging in self-reflection, expanding one's comfort zone, aligning actions with values, and seeking feedback, individuals can gain a deeper understanding of themselves and foster a sense of self-confidence and security. This journey is not a one-time event but a continuous process that requires commitment and perseverance. Through this journey, individuals can uncover their true potential and overcome the limitations that insecurity may impose. Embracing this journey is a transformative experience that can lead to greater self-awareness, personal growth, and a more fulfilling life. In today's society, insecurity is a prevalent issue that many individuals face. Whether it stems from personal experiences, societal pressures, or comparisons to others, overcoming insecurity is crucial for personal growth and self-acceptance. One effective strategy to conquer this pervasive feeling is through cultivating a positive mindset and practicing self-love. By shifting one's focus from negative thoughts and criticisms to embracing individuality and celebrating personal achievements, individuals can develop a stronger sense of self-confidence and overcome their insecurities. Self-compassion plays a significant role in overcoming insecurity. Acknowledging that nobody is perfect and that everyone has flaws allows individuals to embrace their imperfections with kindness and empathy. By treating oneself with compassion and understanding, rather than self-criticism, individuals can break free from the chains of insecurity. Surrounding oneself with a supportive network of friends and loved ones can provide a strong foundation for overcoming insecurity. Building healthy relationships based on trust and respect allows individuals to feel valued and loved for who they are, fostering a sense of belonging and acceptance. This network acts as a safety net, enabling individuals to face their insecurities head-on knowing that they have a support system to rely on. Seeking professional help, such as therapy or counseling, can be instrumental in overcoming insecurity. Therapists provide individuals with the necessary tools and strategies to challenge negative thoughts and beliefs, replacing them with positive and empowering ones. Through guided sessions, individuals can gain a better understanding of the roots of their insecurities and develop effective coping mechanisms for managing and overcoming them. Another important aspect of overcoming insecurity is setting realistic and achievable goals. By breaking down larger goals into smaller, manageable tasks, individuals can build confidence by witnessing their own progress. Each accomplishment becomes a steppingstone towards overcoming insecurities, as individuals realize their own potential and ability to achieve what they set out to do. Practicing self-care and maintaining a healthy lifestyle are crucial components of overcoming insecurity. Engaging in activities that bring joy and fulfillment and prioritizing physical and mental well-being contribute to a positive self-image. Taking care of oneself and engaging in activities that promote self-improvement and growth cultivate a sense of self-worth, making it easier to overcome and silence feelings of insecurity. Overcoming insecurity is a process that requires time, effort, and self-reflection. By adopting a positive mindset, practicing self-love and self-compassion, building a supportive network, seeking professional help, setting achievable goals, and engaging in self-care, individuals can overcome feelings of insecurity and embrace their true selves. It is important to remember that each person's journey towards overcoming insecurity will be unique, and there is no one-size-fits-all solution. By implementing these strategies and embracing personal growth, individuals can develop the necessary tools to conquer insecurity and lead a fulfilling and confident life.

XXV. CONCLUSION

It is clear that overcoming insecurity requires a multifaceted approach. Throughout this essay, we have discussed various strategies that individuals can employ to conquer their insecurities. First and foremost, recognizing and acknowledging the presence of insecurity is crucial. Without this initial step, it becomes difficult to address the root causes and work towards self-improvement. Challenging negative self-talk is essential in combating insecurity. By replacing self-defeating thoughts with positive and affirming statements, individuals can begin to reshape their perception of themselves and build self-confidence. Seeking professional help, such as therapy or counseling, can provide valuable guidance and support in the journey of overcoming insecurity. Therapists can assist individuals in understanding the underlying causes of their insecurities and provide effective coping mechanisms. Cultivating a strong support system of friends and loved ones is vital. Surrounding oneself with supportive and uplifting individuals can greatly contribute to boosting self-esteem and alleviating insecurity. It is important to remember that building self-confidence is a gradual process and may require patience and persistence. Engaging in self-care activities, such as exercise, meditation, or pursuing hobbies, can help individuals focus on their own well-being and promote a sense of self-worth. By prioritizing self-care, individuals can enhance their self-esteem and develop a more positive self-image. Setting realistic goals and celebrating achievements, no matter how small, is crucial in overcoming insecurity.

Each triumph, no matter how insignificant it may seem, is a step forward in building self-assurance and resilience. It is important to remember that everyone experiences insecurity to some degree. It is a normal part of the human experience, and individuals should not be too hard on themselves when faced with moments of insecurity. Instead, individuals should approach these moments as opportunities for growth and self-reflection. Insecurity can serve as a catalyst for personal development and self-improvement. By implementing these strategies and approaches, individuals can embark on a journey towards liberation from the shackles of insecurity. Overcoming insecurity is a deeply personal and transformative process, but with the right mindset and tools, individuals have the power to emerge stronger and more self-assured. It is important to remember that overcoming insecurity is not a destination, but rather an ongoing journey of self-growth and discovery. Through self-reflection, seeking support, self-care, and shifting negative thought patterns, individuals can begin to rewrite their narratives and reclaim their authentic selves. In doing so, they can lead a life filled with confidence, self-acceptance, and resilience.

RECAP OF STRATEGIES TO OVERCOME INSECURITY

Insecurity is a common phenomenon that can adversely affect individuals in various aspects of their lives. There are several effective strategies that can be employed to overcome this deeply-rooted feeling. Firstly, building self-awareness is crucial in dealing with insecurity. Self-awareness allows individuals to recognize and understand their unique strengths and weaknesses. By acknowledging one's capabilities and focusing on personal growth, individuals can boost their self-confidence and reduce feelings of insecurity. Secondly, practicing self-care is essential for combating insecurity. Engaging in activities that promote physical, mental, and emotional well-being can significantly enhance self-esteem and reduce anxiety. This involves adopting a healthy lifestyle, such as eating nutritious food, exercising regularly, getting adequate sleep, and practicing relaxation techniques. Seeking support from trusted individuals is vital for overcoming insecurity. Sharing one's feelings and concerns with loved ones or professionals creates a supportive environment that fosters self-assurance and reassurance. This can be achieved through open conversations, seeking therapy, or joining support groups where individuals can interact with others who share similar experiences. Reframing negative thoughts is a valuable strategy to address insecurity effectively. By replacing self-doubt and negative self-talk with positive affirmations and realistic perspectives, individuals can alter their mindset and develop a more positive self-image. Cognitive-behavioral therapy techniques, such as challenging negative beliefs and substituting them with positive ones, can be instrumental in helping individuals reframe their thoughts. Another effective strategy to overcome insecurity is setting achievable goals. Setting specific, measurable, attainable, relevant, and time-bound (SMART) goals provides individuals with a sense of direction and purpose, helping them to focus their energy and efforts on personal growth. Accomplishing these goals reinforces self-belief and reduces feelings of insecurity. Practicing self-compassion is essential when dealing with insecurity. Instead of harsh self-criticism, individuals should treat themselves with kindness and understanding, just as they would treat a loved one. By recognizing that everyone experiences insecurity at times and forgiving oneself for mistakes and imperfections, individuals can cultivate a sense of self-acceptance and resilience. Overcoming insecurity requires a combination of strategies that address its underlying causes and promote self-confidence and self-acceptance. By building self-awareness, practicing self-care, seeking support, reframing negative thoughts, setting achievable goals, and practicing self-compassion, individuals can navigate through their insecurities and develop a healthier and more confident self-image. It is crucial to remember that overcoming insecurity is a continuous process that requires patience, persistence, and self-reflection. With dedication and the implementation of these strategies, individuals can gradually overcome their insecurities and lead fulfilling lives.

IMPORTANCE OF PERSISTENCE AND SELF-COMPASSION IN THE PROCESS

Persistence and self-compassion play crucial roles in the process of overcoming insecurity. Insecurity can stem from a variety of sources, such as past traumas, societal pressures, or internal self-doubt. To navigate these challenges, individuals must exhibit persistence, as it requires ongoing effort and determination to overcome insecurities that have been deeply ingrained over time. Changing negative thought patterns and developing new coping mechanisms takes time and consistency, making persistence an essential attribute. It allows individuals to remain committed to their growth and pushes them to stay on track even when obstacles arise. Without persistence, individuals may give up on their journey towards self-confidence and fall back into the cycle of insecurity. Self-compassion is key in the process of overcoming insecurity. Insecurities often lead individuals to be harsh and critical towards themselves, perpetuating a negative self-image. Self-com passion involves treating oneself with kindness, understanding, and acceptance, which can counteract the damaging effects of insecurity. By practicing self-compassion, individuals can challenge their self-critical beliefs and develop a more compassionate and affirming perspective. This fosters a sense of self-worth and aids in the process of overcoming insecurity. Persistence and self-compassion intertwine, creating a powerful synergy. Without persistence, self-com passion may remain only as an abstract concept. Individuals need to consistently practice self-compassion in order to internalize and believe in their own self-worth. Similarly, self-compassion drives persistence by providing individuals with the emotional support needed to continue on their journey towards self-confidence. When faced with setbacks, individuals who practice self-compassion are better equipped to dust themselves off and try again, fueling their persistence in the face of adversity. The importance of persistence and self-compassion in the process of overcoming insecurity cannot be overstated. Developing confidence and self-assurance is not an easy task, especially when insecurities have deeply rooted themselves within one's psyche. Persistence enables individuals to remain committed to their growth and push through challenges despite setbacks. It requires individuals to consistently put in the effort and maintain a steadfast mindset, even when faced with moments of doubt. Self-compassion, on the other hand, allows individuals to treat themselves with kindness and understanding, counteracting the damaging effects of insecurity. By fostering self-compassion, individuals can challenge their self-critical beliefs and develop a more positive and affirming self-image. Self-compassion provides individuals with the emotional support needed to persist in the face of adversity, helping them overcome setbacks and continue their journey towards self-confidence. Persistence and self-compassion are paramount in the process of overcoming insecurity. By being persistent, individuals can remain committed to their growth and push through challenges. Self-compassion, on the other hand, helps individuals develop a more positive self-image and provides the emotional support needed to persist. Together, these attributes create a powerful synergy, leading individuals towards greater self-confidence and a more secure sense of self.

Overcoming insecurity is a transformative journey that requires unwavering determination and self-compassion.

ENCOURAGEMENT TO TAKE THE FIRST STEPS TOWARDS A MORE CONFIDENT AND SECURE SELF

Encouragement to take the first steps towards a more confident and secure self is crucial in overcoming insecurity. One effective strategy is setting realistic goals. By establishing clear and attainable objectives, individuals can steadily progress towards building confidence in their abilities. For example, someone feeling insecure about their public speaking skills can set a goal to engage in a small group discussion or deliver a short presentation to a supportive audience. As they achieve these milestones, their confidence will naturally grow. Seeking support from others can be immensely helpful. Connecting with friends, family, or a therapist who can offer encouragement and guidance can provide the necessary reassurance to take those initial steps towards a more secure self. In addition, surrounding oneself with positive influences and individuals who believe in their potential can significantly impact one's self-confidence. By fostering a supportive environment, negative self-perceptions can be replaced with belief in one's capabilities. Engaging in self-reflection and Mindfulness practices can promote self-awareness and understanding, further aiding in the journey towards self-assurance. Regularly taking time to identify and challenge negative thoughts or beliefs can help reframe one's mindset and cultivate a more positive self-image. Similarly, practicing self-compassion is crucial in overcoming insecurity. By treating oneself with kindness and understanding, individuals can build resilience in the face of setbacks and learn to accept imperfections. Taking care of physical health through exercise, proper nutrition, and sufficient sleep can significantly impact one's self-confidence. Regular physical activity not only promotes physical well-being but also releases endorphins, which boost mood and overall self-esteem. Similarly, a healthy and balanced diet can provide the necessary nutrients to support mental and emotional well-being. Stepping out of one's comfort zone and embracing new experiences can be a transformative way to overcome insecurity. By engaging in activities that challenge oneself, individuals can expand their horizons and prove to themselves that they are capable of growth and adaptation. This can be anything from trying a new hobby, pursuing higher education, or traveling to unfamiliar places. Each new experience offers an opportunity for self-discovery and personal growth, ultimately contributing to a more confident and secure self. When individuals are encouraged to take the first steps towards a more confident and secure self, they begin a transformative journey towards overcoming insecurity. Setting realistic goals, seeking support from others, cultivating a supportive environment, engaging in self-reflection and Mindfulness, practicing self-compassion, taking care of physical health, and embracing new experiences are all essential aspects of this process. By incorporating these strategies into their lives, individuals can gradually build the self-confidence needed to overcome insecurities and become their best selves.

BIBLIOGRAPHY

Alexander Chase. 'Insecurity.' How To Overcome Insecurity And Start Embracing Yourself To Increase Your Self-Esteem, Eliminate Anxiety, Jealousy and Procrastination, CreateSpace Independent Publishing Platform, 6/3/2016

Shyla C Wilson. 'Holistic Healing.' Embracing Wellness from Within, Amazon Digital Services LLC Kdp, 5/28/2023

Michael E. McCullough. 'The Psychology of Gratitude.' Robert A. Emmons, Oxford University Press, 2/26/2004

Janet Read. 'Disabled People and the Right to Life.' The Protection and Violation of Disabled People's Most Basic Human Rights, Luke Clements, Routledge, 1/18/2008

Steven Kramer. 'The Progress Principle.' Using Small Wins to Ignite Joy, Engagement, and Creativity at Work, Teresa Amabile, Harvard Business Press, 7/19/2011

John Marshall Reeve. 'Understanding Motivation and Emotion.' John Wiley & Sons, 11/3/2014

Matthew Brighthouse. 'Intp: Understand and Break Free from Your Own Limitations.' Independently Published, 9/25/2017

Harvey B. Milkman. 'Driving With Care: Alcohol, Other Drugs, and Impaired Driving Offender Treatment-Strategies for Responsible Living.' The Participant's Workbook, Level II Therapy, Kenneth

W. Wanberg, SAGE, 11/10/2004

Olivier Serrat. 'Knowledge Solutions.' Tools, Methods, and Approaches to Drive Organizational Performance, Springer, 5/22/2017

Frank Louis Greer. 'The Effectiveness of Avoidance and Non avoidance Coping: a Comparison of Two Types of Stress.' U. of Calif., Davis, 1/1/1983

B. Sanyal. 'Breaking the Boundaries.' A One-World Approach to Planning Education, Springer Science & Business Media, 3/9/2013

Ethan D. Anderson. 'Chemotherapy: A Patient's Guide to Treatment and Recovery.' Born Incredible.com, 1/1/2023

Amara M. Kamara. 'Direct Support from a Manager's Viewpoint.' A Little Day Habilitation Companion, Author House, 6/6/2014

C. Jesse Carlock. 'Enhancing Self Esteem.' Taylor & Francis, 10/8/2013

Patricia C. Broderick. 'Learning to Breathe.' A Mindfulness Curriculum for Adolescents to Cultivate Emotion Regulation, Attention, and Performance, New Harbinger Publications, 6/1/2021

David J. Berghuis. 'The Addiction Progress Notes Planner.' Arthur E. Jongsma, Jr., John Wiley & Sons, 6/5/2009

Martin E. P. Seligman. 'Character Strengths and Virtues.' A Handbook and Classification, Christopher Peterson, Oxford University Press, 4/8/2004

Daniel Goleman. 'Self-Awareness (HBR Emotional Intelligence Series).' Harvard Business Review, Harvard Business Press, 11/13/2018

Health and Medicine Division. 'Preventing Bullying Through Science, Policy, and Practice.' National Academies of Sciences, Engineering, and Medicine, National Academies Press, 9/14/2016

David Ladipo. 'Job Insecurity and Work Intensification.' Brendan Burchell, Psychology Press, 1/1/2002

Osho. 'Fear.' Understanding and Accepting the Insecurities of Life, Macmillan, 10/16/2012

Health and Medicine Division. 'Communities in Action.' Pathways to Health Equity, National Academies of Sciences, Engineering, and Medicine, National Academies Press, 4/27/2017

Robynn Cox. 'Roadmap to a Unified Measure of Housing Insecurity.' SSRN, 1/1/2017